POLICY ESSAY NO. 27

TRADE, ENVIRONMENT, AND THE WTO: THE POST-SEATTLE AGENDA

GARY P. SAMPSON

FOREWORD BY
JAN PRONK
MINISTER FOR HOUSING, SPATIAL PLANNING,
AND THE ENVIRONMENT
GOVERNMENT OF THE NETHERLANDS

DISTRIBUTED BY THE
JOHNS HOPKINS UNIVERSITY PRESS

PUBLISHED BY THE
OVERSEAS DEVELOPMENT COUNCIL
WASHINGTON, DC

Copyright © 2000 by Overseas Development Council, Washington, DC

Distributed by:
The Johns Hopkins University Press
2715 North Charles Street
Baltimore, MD 21218-4319

Library of Congress Cataloging-In-Publication Data

Sampson, Gary P.
    Trade, Environment, and the WTO: The Post-Seattle Agenda/Gary P. Sampson
p. cm. (Policy essay; no. 27)
Includes bibliographical references.
ISBN: 1-56517-029-6
    1. International trade Environmental aspects. 2. Free trade Environmental aspects. 3. World Trade Organization. I. Title. II. Series.

    HF1379 .S253 2000
    382 dc21   00-022542   CIP
    ISBN 1-56517-029-6

Printed in the United States of America.

Publications Editor: Jacqueline Edlund-Braun
Edited by Linda Starke
Cover design: Design Consultants of Virginia

OVERSEAS DEVELOPMENT COUNCIL

Contents

Foreword

In 1979 the Brandt Commission recommended that an "international trade organisation incorporating both GATT and UNCTAD is the objective towards which the international community should work." In the 1990s such a new international trade organization has been established: the World Trade Organization (WTO). The question is to what extent this institution is more than just the previous General Agreement on Tariffs and Trade in a different form, and whether it, in fact, does reflect the concerns that traditionally have been on the agenda of the United Nations Conference on Trade and Development.

The WTO is about more than tariffs and trade. Negotiations within the WTO go beyond tariffs and beyond the industrial sector. Nontariff barriers, agriculture, and services are prominently on the WTO agenda. But in Seattle in late 1999 it became clear that the linkages between trade and development are not yet well established within the new organization. Views differ widely, for example between the largest trading nations in the industrial world and countries in the developing world.

This is no surprise. The relationship between trade and development has been a major issue in international economic deliberations since the establishment of the new international economic order in the 1940s. As a matter of fact, it was also a major issue before then, in economic literature as well as in the practice of trade between rich and poor, empires and colonies, technologically advanced and less developed countries, center and periphery economies, and so on.

Put in more general terms: the relationship between international trade and the social and economic development of nations depends on many factors: size, scale of trade, production structures, economic power, levels of technology, skill levels and educational attainments, natural climate, geography, legal and administrative capacity to set and maintain rules and regulations, and many other factors that vary from nation to nation.

International trade influences domestic processes, in particular in smaller, weaker, and poorer countries. Yet it is also true that domestic structures, mostly those of bigger, stronger, and richer countries, determine the setting of international trade.

To deal with trade in isolation would be futile. Trade cannot be an aim in itself. Nor, in many economies, can it be seen as an independent instrument of economic policy. It is always the relationship that matters: trade and development, trade and finance, trade and investment, trade and competition, trade and labor, trade and technology, trade and environment.

Ignoring these relationships may ultimately mean there will be less trade than many governments, entrepreneurs, and consumers would wish. So not only those whose main interest is trade, but also those who are interested in development, environment, and the quality of life would be wise to deal with all aspects of trade in an integrated manner.

Multilateral trade negotiations will necessarily have to deal with the other issues as well. It is politically impossible today to plead for trade liberalization without at the same time offering policy proposals that address issues or values that will be affected by that liberalization. Without such proposals, further trade liberalization will meet social, economic, and environmental limits and political resistance.

This is the trade agenda for the first decade in the new century. But it will not be possible to deal with all of these issues at the same time. That is too complicated. A way will have to be found to deal with the various relationships in a systematic way, in stages perhaps, or in parallel in different settings, provided that these initiatives are part of an overall effort that proceeds on the basis of generally agreed basic principles.

The WTO can provide a framework for that effort. There is no alternative. But principles and procedures will have to be elaborated in order to reach consensus and to build confidence in the process. Confidence-building can also be sustained by success in a particular area, which then could be translated to other areas as well. Trade and environment issues could offer a promising start. It is an area of conflict, but at the same time it is an area of potential mutual interest. If environmental degradation due to irresponsible economic policymaking produces economic stagnation or decline, trade will suffer. A sustainable environment, however, is conducive to trade.

The same argument would hold for the relationship between trade and development. It has been claimed that economic interdependence and mutual interest form a new basis for successful trade negotiations between industrialized and developing countries. This was a legitimate proposition after the stalemate in the negotiations between North and South in the 1960s and 1970s. But it has not yet led to a breakthrough, maybe because poorer parts of the world are not thought necessary to increase global growth rates or because the richer countries do not fear stagnation.

Environmental concerns are different. Economic decline in a sector due to environmental degradation cannot easily be reversed, unlike economic stagnation due to a lack of investment. Moreover, environmental problems may affect all countries, whether rich or poor.

This offers an opportunity for a breakthrough in negotiations, provided that both the trade community and the environmentalists are aware of their common interests and provided that both sides trust the other side to be aware of this.

Gary Sampson has extensive experience in trade analysis and trade policymaking, as an independent researcher, as a senior official in various international organizations, and as a policy advisor. In this book he presents a lucid analysis of the relationship between trade and environment, followed by a policy agenda within the framework of the WTO. It is an agenda in the interests of all countries, including developing countries. Mutuality is essential. A successful approach in this field may provide us with a model for promising negotiations in other areas where international trade affects domestic processes.

Trade can be good for the environment and for development, but not always and only under certain conditions. A sustainable environment and a sustainable economic development process are good for trade, provided there is consensus about the precise meaning of sustainability. This is the essence of Gary Sampson's Policy Essay: it offers a guide to understanding the implications of sustainability, showing the way toward a mutually supportive, tripartite bond among trade, development, and environment.

Jan Pronk
Minister for Housing, Spatial Planning, and the Environment
Government of the Netherlands
March 2000

Acknowledgments

I would like to thank the staff of the Overseas Development Council for their most professional contribution to the preparation of this essay. In particular, Catherine Gwin for early conversations on the structure of the essay and John Sewell for his continued interest and support. David Weiner provided an invaluable contribution to the substance and drafting of not only this essay, but also of the two ODC Policy Papers that preceded it. The contribution of Jacqueline Edlund-Braun, ODC's Editor, is also appreciated.

This book has benefited enormously from lively conversations with colleagues and friends in government, academia, nongovernmental organizations, and the World Trade Organization, as well as from my participation in numerous conferences and meetings that addressed matters relating to trade, environment, and the WTO.

An earlier version of the manuscript was read in its entirety by Steve Charnovitz, Otto Genee, Richard Snape, and Conrad Von Molkte, all of whom provided constructive and particularly helpful comments. Both Risa Schwartz and Johanna Sampson provided valuable research assistance.

This essay is part of a larger project on the role of the WTO in global governance, which is financed by The Ford Foundation.

■ ■ ■

The Overseas Development Council would like to acknowledge the Charles Stewart Mott Foundation for their generous support of ODC's Project on Environmental Governance, of which this essay is a part. This volume also results from ODC's overall program of research and analysis on multilateral cooperation for development, which was made possible by the support of The Ford Foundation, The John D. and Catherine T. MacArthur Foundation, the Charles Stewart Mott Foundation, and the Rockefeller Foundation. ODC's overall research program also receives support from BankAmerica Corporation, Exxon Corporation, and Ford Motor Company.

ENVIRONMENTALISTS AND THE WTO

■   In January 1995, the World Trade Organization (WTO) became the successor to GATT—the General Agreement on Tariffs and Trade. The new organization was the culmination of years of negotiations aimed at liberalizing world trade and extending the reach of the system that oversees international trade. Among other things, these negotiations also provided for a WTO ministerial meeting to be convened every two years; the third ministerial meeting was held in Seattle at the end of 1999.

Although the importance of protecting the environment is clearly acknowledged in the preamble of the agreement that established the WTO, it was not a main focus of the negotiations.[1] With respect to the environment, the WTO and its associated agreements place no constraints on governments implementing within their borders whatever legitimate policy options they wish. Nevertheless, environmental nongovernmental organizations (NGOs) widely believe that the WTO systematically works against the interests of the environment.

Expressions of dissatisfaction with the WTO on the part of environment and other public interest groups reached new heights during the meeting of ministers in Seattle. Instead of launching the ninth round of multilateral trade negotiations since the late 1940s, the meeting concluded in disarray.

Some of the criticism at Seattle and elsewhere derives from a lack of understanding of the WTO and how it operates. The organization is assailed for alleged sins of commission and sins of omission. Frequently this criticism is made without a clear sense of the responsibilities of the WTO that have been agreed to and accepted by the member governments.[3]

Clearly there is a need to fill this information gap as quickly as possible and to change processes at the national and multilateral levels so as to better inform people about the WTO and its activities.

Useful as this will be, it will not in itself solve the problem. Many critics of the WTO base their complaints and their proposals for reform on a thorough understanding of WTO rules and processes.[4] If the concerns expressed at Seattle are to be addressed and public support for the WTO assured, some way must be found not only to improve public understanding of the WTO, but also to respond to legitimate criticism without severely damaging the organization's usefulness.

In the wake of Seattle, building public support for the WTO is as important today as at any time in the 50-year history of the organization and its predecessor. The eyes of the world are now on the organization, and building public support cannot wait for a new round of negotiations—indeed it is a precondition for launching new negotiations.

. . . .

DEVELOPING COUNTRY CONCERNS

■   IT IS ALSO IMPORTANT AFTER SEATTLE that the WTO better accommodate the concerns of developing countries. These nations see little of advantage to them in many areas of WTO work, not the least being the trade and environment discussions. Because more than 100 of the WTO's members are developing countries, their interests cannot be neglected in an organization where decisions are taken on the basis of consensus. In the past it was sometimes argued that developing country interests were not always clearly identified. If this was ever true, it is no longer the case. In his statement to the High Level Symposium on Trade and Development at the WTO in March 1999, Rubens Ricupero, the Secretary-General of the U.N. Conference on Trade and Development, called for developing countries to become "active protagonists in future negotiations" and for there to be a "pro-active positive agenda" with a "constructive and affirmative strategy in all issues under negotiation."[5] Developing countries were indeed more active in the preparations for the meeting in Seattle than for any other GATT or WTO meeting. The willingness of large numbers of developing countries to stand in the way of a ministerial consensus—a consequence of their perception that they were being excluded from key meetings and that some of their principal negotiating objectives were not being addressed—contributed significantly to the collapse of the Seattle meeting.

. . . .

WINDOW OF OPPORTUNITY

■   THE FAILURE OF THE SEATTLE MINISTERIAL and the forceful expressions of concern by environmentalists before and during that meeting have increased the urgency of addressing constructively the issues that have bedeviled the trade and environment debate for some years. But there are other practical reasons why it is important to push forward this agenda. First, a great deal of groundwork has been done in the NGO community and the WTO to identify and flesh out the most important and contentious issues. In the WTO, members have discussed at length most of the major issues and advanced comprehensive proposals. Similarly, environmentalists have published numerous reports. Efforts to increase mutual understanding were made during the March 1999 High Level Symposium on Trade and the Environment.[6] Representatives of environmental NGOs, intergovernmental organizations, national institutions, and WTO member countries met to exchange views and voice their respective concerns.[7] This was the largest and most comprehensive in a series of meetings of this nature.

In addition, considerable work has been undertaken in the regular bodies of the WTO—including the General Council and the Dispute Settlement Body—to address many of the principal concerns of environmentalists, such as those relating to transparency and improving WTO dispute settlement procedures. Finally, there is growing evidence of a political awareness—clearly expressed by the high-level calls for the Trade and Environment Symposium—of the need to raise public support for the WTO.[8] This is even more evident after Seattle.

If there is indeed a window of opportunity in the post-Seattle period, it can be seized or ignored—and given the current state of play in the trade and environment debate, either scenario is possible. It is hoped that the following chapters will make a contribution to ensuring that the opportunities of the coming months and years are taken advantage of and transformed into positive outcomes.

. . . .

OBJECTIVES AND OUTLINE

■   THE ANALYSIS THAT FOLLOWS IS PREMISED on an understanding of what the WTO, as it is presently structured, can and cannot do, and how change comes about in a consensus-based organization. Only with this information in hand can false expectations be avoided, along with the frustration that has been so evident in the past with the perceived lack of progress in the WTO on trade and environment issues. To achieve this goal, it is important that all the players in any discussions are operating with the same information. Thus, the first objective of this policy essay is to address some of the most critical areas where there may be a lack of information—not only on substance, but also on WTO procedures. Second, it is important to acknowledge the difficulty in advancing ambitious and realistic proposals in the WTO. Even minor changes in WTO rules and processes require consensus decisions on the part of governments at very different levels of economic development and with very different economic interests and social concerns.

In this context, it is important to consider the time and effort necessary to implement any proposed changes. In the WTO, rule change is rare and, in practice, only achieved after extensive negotiation. There are, however, ways to advance the process. The interpretation of rules changes regularly (through panel rulings, for example) and some rules are simply ignored (such as those relating to regional trading agreements). Some processes are in the hands of the Secretariat, require no government approval, and therefore can be implemented quickly (the convening of symposia, for instance, or the creation of a comprehensive WTO Web site). In each instance, the degree of government involvement and—therefore the time horizon for change—differs greatly.

This policy essay has been written in the belief that it is possible to identify the most important issues that must be dealt with in the coming months and years. Without such a blueprint, there could be a further widening of the divide between the trade and environment communities, setting WTO negotiations on the same unfortunate course followed in recent negotiations in the Organisation for Economic Co-operation and Development on the ill-fated Multilateral Agreement on Investment. Enhancing and enriching the dialogue will help avoid that outcome and generate negotiating authority for future negotiations at the national level.

In fact, such a dialogue will make it clear that there are instances in which the WTO can be used constructively by the NGO community to achieve its own goals—instances in which the WTO and NGOs should be partners. In other areas, it becomes apparent that the WTO does not have the solutions sought by NGOs but does have the potential to work in a cooperative manner both with NGOs and with other institutions to build an effective framework for dealing with global environmental problems.

The topics addressed here relate primarily to the concerns expressed by environmental NGOs about WTO activities. Much of what follows, however, is equally relevant for other public interest groups. References to the trade community or trade officials throughout should be read as meaning those who believe that accommodating the demands of environmental NGOs could undermine the proper functioning of the WTO rules-based multilateral trading system. It is important to note, however, that such terms cannot be used in a cut-and-dried manner. There is no reason to believe that officials representing governments at the WTO are any less concerned about the environment than any other cross-section of society, even if they resist trade measures being used for environmental purposes.[9] Similarly, many environmental organizations are as concerned as trade officials are with maintaining the discipline of the multilateral trading system and a rules-based decision-making process.

In the following chapters, I will address some of the key issues that have emerged in the WTO debate on trade and environment and offer policy proposals that can be addressed in the absence of a new round of negotiations. The intention is not to be exhaustive with respect to all the relevant issues, but rather to be illustrative in drawing attention to some of the most important topics on which progress can be made. Because of time and space constraints, I do not directly deal with some of the broader issues relating to sustainable development. Nevertheless, a number of issues are addressed that are highly relevant to the view expressed in the U.N. General Assembly's Special Session in its first five-year review of progress in the implementation of Agenda 21—namely, that the "multilateral trading system should have the capacity to further integrate environmental considerations and enhance its contribution to sustainable development, without undermining its open, equitable and non-discriminatory character."[10]

I also argue throughout that development must become an integral part of the trade and environment debate in the WTO, taking into account the interests and concerns of developing countries. In a consensus-based organization, there will be no progress if the interests of two-thirds of the members are not accommodated or if those countries have a sense of exclusion from the negotiating process. Chapter 2 discusses some of the building blocks that are important for later chapters and proposals. In particular, some of the practical aspects of WTO operations are described, along with the thinking behind some approaches to environment and trade issues. Chapter 3 addresses the recurrent criticism that the WTO is a nontransparent organization and unaccountable to the public at large and makes a number of proposals for improving the present situation. These initiatives could go far in meeting the common concerns of many environmental NGOs, evident at Seattle and elsewhere, without requiring exhaustive negotiations on the part of WTO members.

Chapter 4 provides a clear example of how WTO rules can be used constructively by NGOs to help them achieve what are in many instances objectives that environmentalists have been pursuing for some time. The WTO and NGOs can be allies in removing a number of measures that both harm the environment and stand in the way of expanded exports from developing countries. Chapter 5 stresses that much of the conflict between the trade and environment communities derives from different views on the part of different societies as to what are appropriate standards for protecting health and the environment both at home and abroad. If the WTO continues to find itself in the position of adjudicator in this debate, it will face an impossible task.

Chapter 6 then addresses the question of how multilateral environmental agreements (MEAs) and the WTO can sit together comfortably in a coherent multilateral system. Although this topic was under active discussion in the mid-1990s, efforts to address potential problems stemming from inconsistent rules in the WTO and MEAs seem to have lost their sense of urgency. This is unfortunate, as some of the MEAs currently under negotiation are potentially far more important from a WTO perspective than were earlier ones. Chapter 7 looks at the dispute settlement process at the WTO and the adverse reaction of the environmental community to decisions of the panels and the appellate body in some recent high-profile disputes. And, finally, the concluding chapter makes a number of specific policy proposals, identifies future priorities for the coming years, and suggests how decisions could be arrived at in these priority areas.

The approach here is deliberately nonlegal. Too much policy in the WTO is now formulated on the basis of finding legal "solutions" to problems, often through legal interpretations of the GATT and WTO agreements, instead of through decisions taken by all members after a full-fledged policy debate. Today's WTO is moving toward being a "House of Litigation," lost in the intricacies of legal rulings, rather than an institution based on widely accepted principles that have produced time-tested policies. This needs to change.

[1] The Preamble to the Agreement Establishing the World Trade Organization (WTO) states that members recognize "that their relations in the field of trade and economic endeavor should be conducted with a view to raising standards of living while allowing for the optimal use of the world's resources in accordance with the objective of sustainable development, seeking both to protect and preserve the environment and to enhance the means for doing so." The texts of the agreements can be found in WTO, *The Results of the Uruguay Round Negotiations: The Legal Texts* (Geneva: WTO, 1995).

[2] Although the WTO does not constrain member governments from protecting their environment, it does not have a remit for formulating or enforcing environment policy either nationally or multilaterally.

[3] There are currently 135 governments that belong to the WTO. In what follows, these will be referred to as the WTO members. While the 15 countries of the European Union are individual members, they are represented at WTO meetings (with the exception of the WTO Budget Committee) by the European Commission, which speaks on behalf of the 15 member states. National delegations are frequently made up of officials from the national departments of trade—or sometimes foreign affairs—with specialist representation depending on the subject-matter under discussion (such as treasury officials for financial services negotiations, agriculture officials for the negations on agriculture, and environment officials for meetings of the Committee on Trade and Environment). Resources and other considerations certainly limit the breadth of representation of national administrations in meetings.

[4] Good examples of the detailed knowledge of WTO activities include the extensive review of the various proposals made in the Committee on Trade and Environment. See Kenneth P. Ewing and Richard D. Tarasofsky, *The Trade and Environment Agenda: Survey of Major Issues and Proposals, from Marrakesh to Singapore*, Environment Policy and Law Paper No. 33 (Gland, Switz., and Cambridge, U.K.: World Conservation Union–IUCN, 1997). A similar example is the critique of the WTO International Institute for Sustainable Development (IISD), *The World Trade Organisation and Sustainable Development: An Independent Assessment* (Winnipeg, IISD,Canada: 1996).

[5] See the presentation by the Secretary-General of UNCTAD to the WTO High Level Symposium on Trade and Development, 17–18 March 1999.

[6] For a summary of the proceedings of this meeting, see IISD, WTO High Level Symposium on Trade and the Environment, 15–16 March 1999, *Sustainable Development*, 22 March 1999.

[7] Although a consensus was reached among WTO members to hold the High Level Symposium, the degree of enthusiasm for such a meeting varied greatly, with a number of developing countries expressing the greatest doubts on the grounds that there is little evidence of any benefits for them from such a meeting.

[8] It is reflected in the Quad Ministerial Communiqué of 29–30 April 1998, the Report of the European Parliament adopted on 30 April 1998, and the call by President Clinton for a joint Ministerial Conference of Trade Ministers and Environment Ministers at the celebrations for the 50 years of the Multilateral Trading System in May 1998. The call for a high-level meeting on the part of Leon Brittan, Vice President of the European Commission, is found in Saddrudin

Aga Khan (ed.), *Policing the Global Economy: Why, How and for Whom* (London: Cameron and May, 1998).

[9] Also, some trade officials may well be of the view that accommodating the demands of NGOs will not undermine the proper functioning of the trading system.

[10] United Nations, *Overall Review and Appraisal of the Implementation of Agenda 21: Report of the Ad Hoc Committee of the Whole of the Nineteenth Special Session,* United Nations General Assembly Nineteenth Special Session, A/S-19/29 (New York: United Nations, 27 June 1997), para. 29.

DEMOCRACY AND INCLUSION

■ THE WORLD TRADE ORGANIZATION (WTO) has come under increasing attack from environmentalists and others concerned about globalization and the WTO's alleged lack of concern about sustainable development. Many critics talk about the WTO as if it were an autonomous body with a life and personality of its own. Such a beast does not exist in reality. (See Box 2–1.) The WTO is a collectivity of governments acting on behalf of their constituents in accordance with certain multilaterally agreed principles that have been adopted by consensus. If the WTO is acting against the interests of the environment, it is the collectivity of governments represented in the organization that is doing so. And only governments can change that.

A question frequently raised by NGOs—and increasingly by developing countries—is whether the WTO is a democratic organization. Those who think that it is note that although the organization's procedures are complex, decisions are generally taken on the basis of a consensus of members' views.[1] If democracy means the consent of all members in the decision-making process, they argue, then the WTO is very democratic. Decisions are not taken, and agreements not adopted, until each member is satisfied that the rights it has acquired and obligations it has undertaken are balanced fairly.

Supporting this point of view is the fact that negotiations, such as those undertaken in the context of the Uruguay Round, are by their very nature lengthy; it invariably takes time to accommodate the concerns of all WTO members. Additionally, because the results of decisions are legally binding, it is understandable that governments consider carefully the implications of decisions before their adoption. If democracy means accountability to the public, then it can be further argued that the WTO is indeed democratic. Even after the completion of negotiations involving all WTO members and the acceptance of the outcome by government delegations, what is agreed to still must be ratified according to the domestic parliamentary procedures of each WTO member.

Other observers, however, hold that the WTO is far from democratic. They note, for example, that frequently there are informal meetings in Geneva with very limited participation. This argument was reinforced by the lack of participation of many small developing country delegations in Seattle

Box 2-1. THE MANY FACES OF THE WTO

- The WTO is a set of agreements that create legally binding rights and obligations for all members. So, too, do the schedules for tariffs and other limitations and restrictions on imports of goods and services attached to the respective agreements. These schedules bind the degree of openness of domestic markets to imported goods and services. The agreements and schedules have been negotiated multilaterally and agreed to by all WTO members. Unlike other international agreements, the rights and obligations contained in the agreements are enforced through a dispute settlement mechanism that provides for both compensation and retaliation in cases of noncompliance.

- The WTO is an intergovernmental forum where delegations from member countries meet to discuss and negotiate a number of trade-related matters. In the Trade Policy Review Body, for example, governments periodically review the trade policies of other members. They discuss recent developments in the multilateral trading system. WTO members also negotiate to liberalize trade and to change rules when thought necessary, usually within the context of formal multilateral rounds of negotiations. To date there have been eight such rounds—the most recent one, the Uruguay Round, lasted from September 1986 to December 1993. Its results are embodied in the 30 legal agreements and numerous supplementary decisions signed by ministers from over 100 countries in April 1994 in Marrakesh. The WTO and its agreements entered into force in January 1995.

- The WTO is a relatively small secretariat with neither enforcement powers nor any role in the interpretation of the legal rights and obligations of members. It has a total staff of around 500 and an annual budget of less than $90 million. It is one of the smaller international organizations—dwarfed by the size of the World Bank, United Nations, International Monetary Fund, and numerous other organizations.

- The WTO consists of governments that have agreed not to discriminate against the trade in goods and services of other members, either between supplying countries or between national and foreign suppliers of the same goods and services. Although WTO rules are legally binding, they do not rule out the possibility of members agreeing to forgo their rights by undertaking obligations in other agreements that provide for measures that would otherwise violate WTO rules. Governments may agree to ban trade in endangered species, for instance, when such restrictions on other goods may be prohibited by WTO rules. As an intergovernmental organization, WTO members are presumed to be acting on behalf of the collective interests of their diverse constituents. While governments liberalize trade to secure benefits for the economy as a whole, they are aware that some interests groups may be adversely affected in this process; it is assumed that governments take into account the concerns of all domestic interest groups when they take decisions.

Source: Author.

Ministerial meetings. In such closed meetings, "non-papers" are discussed that many delegations never even see.[2] According to this view, some countries, particularly developing ones, are systematically denied access to information and "excluded" from what are sometimes important negotiations.[3]

When considering this criticism, it is important to draw a distinction between lack of participation in meetings and systematic exclusion of countries from the process. Informal groups do meet frequently in the WTO, particularly when drafting texts. Limited participation is in many instances the most efficient way to proceed; agreements reached in smaller groups of the most concerned countries can later be extended to other, less directly concerned, countries. In such instances, absence is as common for industrial countries as it is for developing ones.[4]

When such groups meet, however, representativeness is important. In any informal consultations, if the Chairman is present, there should, in principle, always be representation from all the different groups that have an interest in the matter under discussion. A competent Chairman will know that it is in his interest to try to ensure that any country with a particular interest that cannot attend an informal consultation will be represented by a country with a similar interest. Without this assurance, consensus could be blocked at a later stage by countries that were excluded from the meeting or that did not see their interests reflected in the outcome. It is in fact the responsibility of the member representing the interests of others—or of the Chairman—to keep other members informed. The success or otherwise of this process is very much in the hands of the Chairman, be it a meeting of ministers in Seattle or a much less important meeting in Geneva.

Notwithstanding the importance of a consultative process in which interests are broadly represented, developing countries are indeed systematically absent from not only informal but also formal meetings. This non-participation, however, is frequently only the symptom of a broader problem, the source of which is a lack of resources and expertise to service the negotiating process. In the increasingly frequent, complex, and resource-intensive negotiations at the WTO, most small delegations do not have the necessary resources, either in Geneva or at home, to service the negotiating process and participate meaningfully.[5] Many small nations do not have a representative in Geneva, which makes even partial participation in the WTO process almost impossible. The increased participation of many developing countries can only come about with a strengthening of their human and institutional capacity to participate in the WTO process. This, in turn, is only possible if resources are made available for technical assistance and training. In this respect, the regular WTO budget is far from adequate.[6]

For some, democracy means not only governmental representation in meetings but also accountability to the public at large during negotiations. Thus another criticism leveled at the WTO is that domestic parliaments are not part of the process until they are asked to ratify an agreement. A study of 30 countries revealed that parliaments are rarely briefed with respect to the general work of the WTO and are seldom involved in the formulation of the negotiating mandate or guidelines.[7] Members of parliament rarely attend WTO sessions, and the involvement of parliaments in the ratification process is typically either a formality or nonexistent.[8]

Finally, if democracy means that each WTO member has the same power in the process, then the WTO is far from democratic. The more economically powerful countries clearly have greater influence. And because decisions are made by consensus, frequently achieved through the exchange of concessions, powerful countries have far more bargaining chips to use in terms of offering trade-offs and eventually leveraging less powerful countries into "agreeing" on the preferred "consensus decision."

. . . .

TRADE POLICY AND THE ENVIRONMENT: SOURCES OF CONFLICT

■ IT HAS BEEN ARGUED THAT THERE IS A NATURAL or built-in potential for conflict between trade policy and policies relating to the environment. Examples of such conflict include the following:

■ higher environmental standards in an importing country than in an exporting one, leading to a loss of international competitiveness for certain industries in the importing country and pressure for a lowering of environmental standards to gain back market share;

■ weakly regulated pollution havens that attract foreign direct investment;

■ compensatory border adjustment measures to offset environmentally driven taxes or subsidies conflicting with trade rules;

- trade liberalization and economic growth leading to resource depletion and environmental degradation;

- cross-border pollution or damage to the global commons, with trade sanctions that break WTO rules used as retaliatory measures;

- disguised protection through the use of domestic standards tailored to discriminate against imports;

- conflicting obligations in multilateral environmental agreements (MEAs) and WTO trade agreements; and

- eco-labeling acting as a barrier to trade.

A great deal of excellent material has been written about all these topics.[9] This section will not cover these specific issues in detail, but rather will flag some basic differences in the approach to policy formulation in the areas of environment and multilateral trade—differences that lie at the heart of this debate.

Much of the conflict involves disagreement over the nature and extent of government intervention. Designing appropriate government intervention has a long history in trade theory and practice. Two hundred years ago, David Ricardo demonstrated that it is in the interests of two countries to trade, even if one country could produce all goods m᠁e cheaply than the other—even, in other words, if it has an absolute advantage in the production of all goods. With a simple numerical example, Ricardo showed that the country without any absolute advantage has a comparative advantage in some goods, and that these can be profitably traded.[10] Goods with a potential comparative advantage are those in which the opportunity costs of production (the resources forgone in their production) are relatively less than for the trading partner.[11]

The simple logic of comparative advantage has been a driving force behind many powerful policy decisions, ranging from Ricardo convincingly arguing for the removal of the Corn Laws in England in the early part of the nineteenth century to the adoption of outward-oriented development strategies in developing countries over the last few decades. Even though the principle of comparative advantage is widely accepted and underpins the philosophy of an open and liberal trading system, it is viewed by many with considerable mistrust.[12] Their skepticism is directed at the important condition that resources will naturally flow to sectors where there exists a comparative advantage as long as distortions are not introduced by governments. Ricardo—like many other classical economists—argued that countries were generally best served by removing barriers to international trade. The concern of some critics is that the unfettered functioning of comparative advantage can undermine the welfare of society. Market prices may well fail to capture the effects of environmentally damaging activities, for example, and send misleading signals regarding the appropriate use of environmental resources. Resource misallocation due to inappropriate relative price structures can undermine effective environmental management. There may be a failure by the producer to shoulder the costs of environmental degradation borne by society, or inappropriate natural resource depletion because pricing fails to reflect scarcity value. Since these are conditions under which international trade can promote environmentally destructive production, there are calls to limit trade, even though it is production or consumption that causes the problem, not trade as such.

These simple facts go far in explaining much of the difference in approach to policy formulation in the trade and environmental arenas. Many policies designed to protect the environment are based on government intervention through regulation of production activities—for example, through taxes, quantitative restrictions, and subsidies. GATT and the WTO, in contrast, have a long tradition of negotiating away government measures that affect trade (e.g., subsidies affecting exports, export bans, restrictions on imports).[13] Members of the trade community may well argue that environmental degradation associated with trade liberalization is not bad trade policy, but bad environmental management. (See Chapter 4.) If market prices do not reflect the cost to society of damage to the environment, then these costs should have been internalized through effective environmental management.

Another fundamental difference concerns the grounds on which products can be discriminated against during production and marketing. This consideration will permeate much of the discussion here. As noted earlier, the WTO does not inhibit governments from protecting (as they wish) against damage to the environment resulting from the manufacture and consumption of goods produced and used within national boundaries. Final products can be taxed and other charges levied for any purpose thought to be appropriate. Similarly, there are no problems from a WTO perspective with governments levying taxes according to the process used to produce something within their own territory. But the understanding behind a number of WTO agreements is that this flexibility extends only to regulation of domestic products and processes, not the processes used to produce imported products. It does not extend to the extraterritorial application of measures relating to production processes in exporting countries.[14] Mandatory standards may be applied domestically, for example, to limit the use of energy in production processes, but an imported product cannot be discriminated against only because the production process was energy-intensive.[15] In other words, imported products that are physically the same as domestically produced ones are considered to be "like" domestic products irrespective of how they were produced.

The underlying thesis is that should any country wish to influence the manner in which goods are produced in other countries—regardless of how appropriate it may seem to citizens in the importing country—it should not seek to do so through discriminatory trade measures.[16] In general, WTO rules treat products that have the same physical form as "like" products even if they have been produced in very different ways.[17] From the perspective of the environment, environmentally unfriendly goods and services—and the processes that produce them—are categorically different from environmentally friendly ones. Thus while the rationale for environmental regulation is to make discrimination between goods and services mandatory (based, for example, on life-cycle analysis), the rationale for WTO rules is to avoid it as far as imports are concerned.

Most notably, WTO members are bound to grant to the products of other members treatment no less favorable than that accorded to the products of any other country. Thus no member is to give special trading advantages to another or to discriminate against a particular product because of the manner in which it was produced. GATT also stipulates that once goods have entered a market, they must be treated no less favorably than equivalent domestically produced goods.[18]

Here lies the source of one of the fundamental concerns of developing countries in the WTO, and not only on matters relating to the environment.[19] In the view of these nations, permitting discrimination among imports on the basis of production methods would profoundly undermine a principle that lies at the heart of the WTO legal system. This concern manifests itself in a resistance to any attempts to provide for the extension of industrial country production standards to developing countries in order for their exports to be acceptable for import in industrial countries. The strength of feeling on this matter on the part of many developing countries cannot be overstated and was recently evident in the discussion of an appellate body ruling (see Chapter 7) that appeared to leave the question open.[20] It was demonstrated even more dramatically during the Seattle Ministerial, when President Clinton linked trade sanctions to labor standards. Dealing with attempts to discriminate on the basis of production methods has the potential to turn constructive debates looking for solutions into damage limitation exercises on the part of most WTO members (that is, developing countries). If environmentally unfriendly production methods or unacceptable labor or human rights standards become grounds for restricting trade, the door will be open to protectionist abuse, irrespective of how justified the concerns are. This possibility raises the question of not only what standards are in fact appropriate for other countries to adopt, but who has the right to set and enforce them.

In this respect, two particularly important issues are at stake that extend well beyond the usual motivation for applying protectionist measures. First, in some areas much of the desire to restrict imports on the grounds of how they were produced in the exporting country is driven not by protectionist forces but by well-meaning and highly motivated groups from a variety of social sectors. This makes the business of governments in dealing with such groups far more complicated than if the sole motivation were commercial advantage.

The second issue relates to the question of whether the well-meaning groups—notwithstanding their honest motivations—are the holders of the truth with respect to how social and other noneconomic matters are to be dealt with in other countries. And in any event, is it the role of the WTO to enforce the preferred standards of others multilaterally? In very practical terms, it has become clear that many developing countries are concerned about changing WTO procedures to permit trade to be a vehicle for influencing how domestic goods are produced from an environmental perspective. They fear that such measures would be an encroachment on their national sovereignty—and only a step away from including standards relating to labor conditions and other social matters in trade agreements.[21]

Another fundamental difference between trade and environmental policy would appear to lie in the transparency with which the policies themselves are formulated. The environmental community appears to favor openness and transparency in policy formulation, but this has not been GATT and WTO practice in the past. The closed nature of trade negotiations can arguably be traced to the realities of the political economy of protection. The vast literature on this topic makes clear that distributional coalitions form to resist policy change that is not in the interest of certain coalition members. As interest groups can be adversely affected through the process of trade liberalization, they naturally use their influence to resist such change. WTO members—and GATT contracting parties before them—often need to take decisions that are not in the interest of all groups in society but are nevertheless thought to be in the interests of the constituencies that the governments represent when elected democratically. This has very practical implications for governments that spill over into transparency considerations. If, for example, saving an efficient domestic motor vehicle manufacturing industry requires removing tariff protection for a highly protected and inefficient local steel industry, it is most unlikely that the government concerned would invite steel and car manufacturers to the multilateral negotiating table. After reviewing the evidence before it at the national level—and in the case of some countries, holding transparent national public hearings—the government would be expected to take decisions at the multilateral level that were in the interests of the community at large.

A democratically elected government advancing community-wide interests through trade liberalization that may adversely affect individual interest groups may well wish to proceed in a nontransparent manner. Thus many GATT documents have traditionally been kept far from the eyes of the public. National proposals for tariff reductions, for example, continue to be among the most tightly restricted documents during rounds of trade negotiations. As a result, GATT contracting parties in the past have built up a tradition of jealously guarding the intergovernmental character of GATT without the active participation of interested (industry) groups—and the WTO continues the tradition.[22]

Yet another fundamental difference stems from what has been described as the different approaches to trade and environmental rule-making and enforcement. Experience has shown that formal changes to GATT and WTO rules are rare.[23] Since the establishment of the GATT in 1948, there have been only two amendments—one in 1955 and another in 1964.[24] GATT and WTO rules, however, have proved to be very flexible instruments, with "changes" achieved through techniques that have ranged from simple nonenforcement to a variety of relatively informal deviations from rules. It has been argued, for example, that the ambiguity of the final decisions taken by WTO members in certain agreements represents a practical solution to issues or disputes on which it is not possible to reach total agreement. The reasoning is that trade ministries have a certain degree of mutual trust allowing them to leave long-term answers open while short-term pragmatic solutions are found. They are confident that there is enough common interest among members to make it likely that something will be worked out in the long run.[25] Another possibility is that given the contractual nature of WTO agreements, members will only agree to a rule change if the outcome is clear and without risk. Unlike many environmental agreements, the dispute settlement process, with its threat of retaliation and compensation, is a Damocles' sword hanging over those that have to live with the interpretation of the new rules.

The WTO's affinity for ambiguous solutions to legal issues does not seem to provide a solution to the trade and environment debate. In reality, options for addressing the problems environmentalists have with WTO rules have been couched in terms of two rather rigid alternatives: 1) the need for formal decisions involving amendments or waivers; or 2) changes to and interpretation of rules through the dispute settlement procedures. Environmentalists resist the pragmatic, common solutions to the disputes over the meaning of rules—for example, constructive ambiguity in the formulation of text to keep negotiations proceeding—believing that trade ministries do not share the same ultimate values as they do. They therefore do not trust the WTO to achieve a solution for them over the long run.[26]

A further practical consideration is that change in WTO rules is likely to be resisted by those who believe that first GATT and now the WTO have been successful over the past half-century within their own trade mandate. The reduction of barriers to trade in the postwar period has been dramatic, and the concepts, principles, and rules behind the legally binding rights and obligations apply to thousands of billions of dollars of goods and services traded among member countries at all levels of development.[27] The WTO is also apparently popular with many governments of countries in transition and developing nations; over 30 such countries are in the process of trying to join the WTO, not to gain transfers in the form of financial assistance but rather to voluntarily limit their national policy choices in many areas of commerce by trading according to legally binding rules in a nondiscriminatory fashion.

Further support comes from the growing body of evidence that the trade liberalization negotiated within the context of the GATT and the WTO leads to economic growth. The WTO Secretariat surveyed a variety of quantitative studies of the income and trade gains as a result of the Uruguay Round commitments.[28] The survey concluded that there will be a global increase of some 1 percent of annual gross domestic product due to the Uruguay Round.[29] By 2005, this translates into an expected annual global income gain of $250–350 billion (in 1992 dollars).[30] Many empirical studies over the past decades have also demonstrated a positive correlation between liberal trade regimes, higher productivity, and more efficient allocation of resources, and have shown that open, outward-oriented economies have grown more rapidly than closed, inward-looking ones.[31]

The majority of WTO members believe that the rules-based liberal trading system has served them well. The growth in exports of developing countries as a group has been impressive in recent years.[32] Not surprisingly, the participation of developing countries in WTO negotiations has also increased greatly.[33] Twenty-five developing countries took part in the Kennedy Round of negotiations (1964–67), 68 in the Tokyo Round (1973–79), and 76 in the Uruguay Round (1986–93).[34]

The important point here is not to sing the praises of the multilateral trading system but rather to underscore the resistance that can be expected to any fundamental change in the role of the WTO. This resistance has to be factored into proposals for major reform of the functioning of the WTO, particularly because it is an institution where change only comes through consensus decision-making.

· ·

MULTILATERAL TRADE RULES AND MULTILATERAL ENVIRONMENT RULES

■ THERE HAS BEEN A GREAT DEAL OF DISCUSSION in the WTO, in other intergovernmental organizations, and in the NGO community about the relationship between WTO agreements and the many MEAs, a number of which contain trade provisions. The focus tends to be on the possibility of conflict between the rules of trade and environmental agreements. I take up this important topic in detail in Chapter 6, while in this section I focus on how the WTO organizes its work relating to the various trade agreements and compare this with the way environmental agreements are addressed.

The motivation behind this discussion is to respond to the frequent calls for a "framework" within which environmental agreements can be dealt with coherently, effectively, and efficiently. An "architecture" to deal with the various environmental agreements has been called for, and recently WTO Director-General Ruggerio stated his view that environmentalists should "put their house in order." He also made clear that in his view, a "World Environment Organization" could be considered as a means to bring this order.[35]

Because the WTO already exists—young as it may be—comparisons between the multilateral trade system and MEAs may be insightful. This section does not promote one model over another, but instead points to similarities and differences between multilateral agreements that are not administered by a world organization and those that are.

As with multilateral trade agreements, there are a large number of MEAs.[36] The trade agreements are attached to the Agreement Establishing the WTO, which has four annexes. The first contains all the multilateral trade agreements administered by the WTO—the updated GATT of 1947 (that is, GATT 1994)[37] plus 12 other agreements, differing greatly in nature and subject-matter. Some relate to sectors (agriculture, textiles), some to government measures (subsidies, safeguards) or private actions (dumping), and some to processes (import licensing, rules of origin). The annex also contains the General Agreement on Trade in Services (covering trade in all services such as financial, telecommunications, professional, and transport services) and the agreement on Trade-Related Aspects of Intellectual Property Rights (patents, copyrights, trademarks, industrial designs, geographical indications, and so on).[38]

In at least one sense, there is a great deal of similarity between the trade and the environmental agreements—namely the diversity of the subject-matter. Protecting endangered species is very different from pro-tecting the ozone layer, maintaining a stable climate, preserving wetlands, or inhibiting the encroachment of deserts. So it is with trade agreements: quar-antine measures, patents, financial services, dumping, and agricultural price supports are all very different, but nevertheless they, too, are all covered by multilateral trade agreements. Another similarity is that the secretariats that service the environmental agreements are very small, in many cases just five or six people.[39] This is also the case in the WTO, where small divisions service each trade agreement.

Beyond these similarities, however, there is a parting of the ways. Most notably, perhaps, is that trade agreements are dealt with in the same geographical location under the "same roof" in Geneva. The environmental agreements are dealt with by geographically dispersed secretariats in Geneva, Montreal, Nairobi, Bonn, and elsewhere. This presumably has implications for the coherence of the diverse environmental agreements and the effectiveness with which they can be managed. The more than 70 councils, committees, working parties, and other bodies that meet regularly at the WTO building to deal with trade agreements are frequently serviced by the same people, both from national delegations and from the WTO Secretariat. They too, of course, meet under the same roof. In this manner, a high degree of expertise is built up all around, and there is a minimum of travel in servicing the various trade agreements for local delegations stationed in Geneva.

The WTO is a "member-driven" intergovernmental organization: all decisions relating to policy are taken by members. Unlike some other organizations (such as the Bretton Woods institutions), the Director-General has very limited powers. He cannot, for example, formulate policy for the WTO, nor is he expected to comment on the policies of member governments. The power to create, interpret, and enforce rules lies solely in the hands of governments; in this respect, the supreme body of the WTO—the Ministerial Conference—is all important. It has full "authority to take decisions on all matters under any of the multilateral trade agreements."[40] Because ministers meet relatively infrequently (every two years is formally provided for), the functions of the Ministerial Conference are exercised by the General Council, which is also made up of the full membership of the WTO.

In practical terms, the General Council is responsible for the continuing management of the WTO and supervises all aspects of the WTO's activities. In this respect, the organization of work relating to the various multilateral trade agreements differs significantly from that on the environment. There is no such council dealing with the totality of MEAs. Another marked difference is that all of the multilateral trade agreements and the WTO itself have only one chief executive officer—the WTO Director-General. In contrast, there is no common head of the various MEA secretariats.

That governments act collectively with respect to all multilateral trade agreements provides considerable flexibility to a number of aspects of the work of the WTO—most notably, those relating to one of its principal roles, that of a negotiating body. Although not all proposals, initiatives, and even agreements are popular with all members, the collective nature in which they are addressed permits governments to strive for not only a balance of rights and obligations across members, but also a balance of interests. There can be trade-offs among the different agreements. If a government does not find a proposal attractive in one area, it can be "paid off" with something it sees as attractive in another area or agreement.

The frameworks within which trade agreements operate have at least two important features that provide the glue that holds them together. The first is the dispute settlement process. This lies at the heart of the WTO. In all the diverse multilateral trade agreements, breaking the rules means being taken to court; if the offending measures are not brought into conformity with WTO rules, then compensation and retaliation—with the approval of the General Council—are provided for. And in this context, the interrelationships among the trade agreements is critical. Compensation can be sought in the form of improved market access in any of the areas covered by multilateral trade agreements, not just the agreement in which the breach of obligations was committed. Similarly, retaliation can take place in any area covered by the agreements.

Building this effective dispute settlement process required 50 years of experience, however. It is therefore important to be realistic about the WTO model being applied to the MEAs, if indeed that were thought desirable.

This leads to the second important feature of the trade agreements. They are built on the same very simple theoretical foundation—the benefits of international trade.[41] The virtue of progressive liberalization in trade in goods and services is well accepted by members, as is the 200-year-old principle of comparative advantage. The belief that a liberal trading system should operate in a predictable and stable manner is reflected in the commitment to a rules-based system. Regulations affecting trade (tariffs, for example) should be transparent and there should be an effective compliance mechanism. In an operational sense, nondiscrimination appears as a cornerstone of almost all trade agreements.

Although protection of the environment is certainly a common objective of multilateral environmental agreements, it may be that the same opportunity does not exist to apply similar concepts, principles, and rules across the different agreements. Nevertheless, there is no doubt that there is room for greater coherence among the agreements.[42] The WTO, far from perfect as it is, may provide one model for a World Environment Organization, but it is important to caution against attempts to replicate the model. Nevertheless, the WTO does provide a useful yardstick against which the relationships among the environmental agreements can be compared.

THE COMMITTEE ON
TRADE AND ENVIRONMENT

■   A NUMBER OF EVENTS DREW ATTENTION to trade and environmental issues in the GATT and the WTO in the early 1990s. Of primary importance were the 1992 U.N. Conference on Environment and Development in Rio and the very unpopular—at least with environmentalists—GATT Panel Reports on the tuna-dolphin cases. These concerns arose after the launching of the Uruguay Round negotiations, and the trade-environment connection did not find a place on that agenda. Nevertheless, discussions toward the end of the round led to a Ministerial Decision on Trade and Environment (adopted in Marrakesh in April 1994) calling for the creation of a Committee on Trade and Environment (CTE).

The committee was established by the WTO General Council in January 1995. It includes all WTO members and a number of observers from intergovernmental organizations. There are no observers from NGOs, despite a number of requests to be included. The CTE reports to the General Council and is mandated to recommend whether any modifications of the multilateral trading system are required to permit a positive interaction between trade and environmental measures.

The CTE has a standing agenda and meets formally at least twice a year.[43] The committee addresses the relationship between the provisions of the multilateral trading system and trade measures for environmental purposes—in particular, the relationship between WTO rules and compliance procedures and those of the multilateral environmental agreements.[44] Environmental charges, taxes, standards, technical regulations, and packaging, labeling, and recycling requirements used for environmental purposes are addressed, along with their implications for the multilateral trading system. The transparency of trade measures used for environmental purposes is also an agenda item.

One item that has been discussed a great deal is the possibility of gaining environmental benefits through removing trade restrictions and distortions in industrial countries, particularly those impeding the exports of developing countries. The discussion has been restricted to environmental benefits of increased imports in the industrial country and has not extended to the possible environmental damage of expanded exports from the developing country. (See Chapter 4 for an elaboration of this.) This is because developing countries do not want to face opposition to their exports on the grounds that the products or production processes could be environmentally harmful according to standards established outside their borders. Other matters addressed relate to problems surrounding the export of domestically prohibited goods, whether additional environmental provisions should be written into the General Agreement on Trade in Services, and the significance for the environment of various provisions of the Agreement on Trade-Related Aspects of Intellectual Property Rights. The committee has also discussed the appropriate arrangements for relations with intergovernmental and NGOs referred to in the Agreement Establishing the WTO.[45]

The April 1994 Ministerial Decision called on the CTE to report to the first biennial meeting of the Ministerial Conference, which would review its work and terms of reference in light of its recommendations. This report was heavily negotiated, forwarded to Ministers, and adopted in Singapore in December 1996.[46] It summarized the discussions of the CTE since its establishment, as well as the conclusions it had reached.

Many people fought hard in support of the creation of the CTE, and expectations were high that it would find solutions to many of the problems emerging through what seemed to be a conflict of interests in the formulation of trade and environmental policy. Yet the culmination of the first two years of its work—the Report to Ministers in Singapore—has been roundly criticized, as have many other aspects of its work.[47] The committee has been accused of, among other things, failing in its task of recommending modifications to the provisions of the multilateral trading system "to enhance a positive interaction between trade and environmental measures and for the promotion of sustainable development."

This criticism seems in large measure misplaced. In fact, it could be argued that the committee has done what it was asked to do quite satisfactorily. The negative perception has several sources. For one thing, the report to the Singapore meeting contains many policy conclusions that are not expressed as such. One example is the conclusion that environmental policy should not be left to trade officials, but to those who have the appropriate expertise—both nationally and internationally. This means that while the relevant national authorities should have total discretion as to their domestic environmental policies, by far the best way to deal with transboundary environmental problems is to develop standards and compliance mechanisms in the context of MEAs. (See Chapter 6.) Increasing interaction with MEA secretariats through their presence at meetings of the CTE, and the greater understanding WTO trade officials now have of these agreements, may well be one main reason why no trade-related measure taken under an MEA has been brought to the WTO disputes settlement process.

The negative opinion about the CTE may also in part be explained by the fact that many of the high-profile concerns of environmentalists cannot be dealt with in the committee. They are simply not within its terms of reference. Nevertheless, the CTE has been expected to resolve these problems. One example of where change is being sought is the dispute settlement process (where, for example, environmentalists have argued for permission to submit amicus briefs to panels dealing with the environment). These matters are the responsibility of bodies other than the CTE, however. So, too, with the issue of derestriction of documents and many other aspects of increased transparency that are dealt with in the General Council.

Finally, the failure of the CTE to take the decisions that some expected of it may in reality be an indication of the complexity of the issues in hand and the respect of WTO officials for this complexity. The time spent in discussions provides support for the view that the WTO is not a body that overrides environmental considerations in the pursuit of free trade. Quite the contrary. The CTE report in December 1996 makes clear that WTO members do not want a role in environmental policymaking and enforcement, nor do they take lightly changing rules that could give them this role.

Indeed, if the report of the CTE to ministers in Singapore is looked at constructively, it can be viewed as an indispensable piece of background work needed for moving the process forward following the meeting in Seattle. What is needed now is the political will to take the necessary decisions.

In this respect, an important question is what should be the future role—if any—of the CTE. I will return to this question on several occasions in the following chapters. At this stage, it is perhaps appropriate to propose that the CTE itself examine what further work needs to be done to complete the tasks originally assigned to it by ministers in Marrakesh in April 1994. At a minimum, it would seem appropriate that, on the basis of five years of experience, the committee take stock of what has been accomplished. If more work needs to be done, then this should be completed. But it is not difficult to imagine that little work remains to be done in terms of the existing agenda. If this is the case, then the CTE could be either wound up or given a new role that would better serve present needs. This point will be taken up in Chapter 8.

....

PRIORITIZING REFORMS

■ ANY PROPOSALS FOR REFORMING THE WTO must take into account the special nature of the organization. It is worth remembering that many governments will be loathe to modify rules, and that there are some fundamentally different approaches to the formulation of environmental and trade policies. This clearly points to a need for close coordination and collaboration on the part of government officials responsible for trade policy and environmental policy (another conclusion of the CTE report to ministers).

Given the manner in which the WTO operates, it would seem reasonable to divide issues that need to be addressed and possible outcomes into three categories, depending on the degree of government involvement or negotiation. The first are objectives that can be achieved if there is enough informal support for the Director-General to take the necessary steps without formal discussion and decisions on the part of the members; in such cases consultation is important, but not negotiation. A second group involves initiatives that require the collective approval of members but not necessarily changes in rules, rights, or obligations. Each WTO member has joined the organization because the existing balance of rights and obligations is seen to be satisfactory. Upsetting this balance may require negotiation in areas that may be quite outside those under discussion. But there have been plenty of cases in which members operating expeditiously within the existing framework of rules have achieved certain objectives. The deal struck at the Singapore Ministerial on information technology provides a good example. Third, some objectives can only be met through a change in rules. The procedures for changing rules in the WTO are complex. In practical terms, achieving these objectives requires a more comprehensive round of trade negotiations, during which cross-sectoral trade-offs are possible.

NOTES

[1] For an explanation of how decisions are taken in the WTO, see John Jackson, *The World Trade Organization: Constitution and Jurisprudence*, Chatham House Papers (London: Royal

Institute of International Affairs, 1998), Section 3.4. See also John H. Jackson, "Global Economics and International Economic Law," *Journal of International Economic Law,* Vol.1, No. 1(March 1998).

[2] It is also argued that the WTO is nondemocratic because of the lack of participation by non-governmental representatives. This aspect of the debate is discussed later in this chapter as well as in Chapter 3.

[3] See Martin Khor, in Saddrudin Aga Khan (ed.), *Policing the Global Economy: Why, How and for Whom* (London: Cameron and May, 1998), p. 194.

[4] Of course, as in any negotiations, groups of countries may meet privately of their own volition to discuss common interests, and choose whom they wish to have present. This is a normal procedure and no one can deny them this right.

[5] The Egyptian delegation to the WTO has estimated that there were 2,847 meetings in the WTO in 1997, or an average of 10 meetings per working day. See *Communication from Egypt,* High Level Symposium on Trade and Development, mimeo (Geneva: WTO, 17 March 1997).

[6] In the 1998 regular budget of the WTO, only $500,000 was provided for technical cooperation and training. This constitutes approximately $5,000 per developing-country member.

[7] Christophe Bellmann and Richard Gerster, "Accountability in the World Trade Organization," *Journal of World Trade,* Vol. 30, No. 6 (December 1996).

[8] The same study proposed the establishment of a WTO Parliament composed of Members of Parliament of national states to guarantee a direct line to those bodies and to tackle an entire series of international problems. It is difficult to imagine all WTO members agreeing to establish such a body. Further, this could be seen as an example of WTO members being expected to resolve problems collectively at the multilateral level when solutions lie at the national level.

[9] See, for example, Dan Esty, *Greening the GATT* (Washington, DC: International Institute for Economics, July 1994), and Duncan Brack (ed.), *Trade and Environment: Conflict or Compatibility?* (London: Royal Institute of International Affairs and Earthscan, 1997).

[10] Writing in the early part of the nineteenth century, David Ricardo reasoned that "A country enabled to manufacture commodities with much less labor that her neighbors may, in return for such commodities, import a fraction of the corn required for its consumption, even if corn could be grown with much less labor than in the country from which it was imported." See R. M. Hartwell, "Introduction," in *D. Ricardo: The Principles of Political Economy and Taxation,* (U.K: H. Watson & Viney Ltd., 1971).

[11] Teachers normally convince their students of the common sense of the principle of comparative advantage with an example along the lines of a neurosurgeon employing an administrative assistant to run the office even if the surgeon is more efficient in both surgery and office management. With the (less well paid) assistant releasing the (highly paid) resources of the surgeon to perform the professional tasks, it is profitable for the surgeon to employ the assistant, spending more time doing what the surgeon has a comparative advantage in doing, and benefitting in the process.

[12] In his Presidential address to the Congress of the International Economics Association in Montreal in 1969, Nobel laureate Paul Samuelson remarked that the Ricardian theory of

comparative advantage was the one proposition in all the social sciences that was both true and nontrivial.

[13] The GATT and WTO have certainly been less than pure in negotiating away all varieties of barriers to trade. The Multifibre Arrangement is an example of the GATT providing legal cover for quantitative restrictions on imported textiles and clothing from developing countries.

[14] As will be seen in Chapter 7, this is less clear after the appellate body ruling on the shrimp-turtle dispute.

[15] This point is further developed in the discussion on the Technical Barriers to Trade Agreement in Chapter 5.

[16] See Richard H. Snape, *Trade and Multilateral Trade Agreements: Effects on the Global Environment*, TASMAN Institute Conference, Canberra, 15–16 March, 1994, mimeographed.

[17] Exceptions to the rules include certain instances where "like" goods are produced with subsidies or without meeting specified standards with respect to the protection of intellectual property rights.

[18] The exceptional circumstances under which discrimination is provided for in WTO rules is discussed in Chapter 6.

[19] For a clear statement of these and other concerns of developing countries, see Magda Shahin, "Trade and Environment; How Real is the Debate," in Gary P. Sampson and W. Bradnee Chambers (eds.), *Trade, Environment and the Millennium* (Tokyo: United Nations University Press, 1999).

[20] See the remarks by a number of developing countries in WTO, *Minutes of Meeting of the Dispute Settlement Body*, WT/DSB/M/50 (Geneva: WTO, 14 December 1998), discussing the shrimp-turtle dispute, where it was argued that dictating fishing practices in other countries was an encroachment on national sovereignty.

[21] In the meeting of the Dispute Settlement Body referred to earlier, concern with the extension of such precedents to labor standards was clearly expressed.

[22] A corollary of this is that the GATT has historically paid a great deal more attention to defending itself in terms of the conventional political economy of protection than in dealing with interest groups concerned with the environment. It could be added that while environmental concerns in the trade arena are not new, the intensity of the concern is relatively recent. For example, trade and environment was not an issue in the formulation of the agenda for the Uruguay Round.

[23] See Jackson, *The World Trade Organization*, op. cit. note 1.

[24] There were, however, understandings negotiated in the Uruguay Round relating to some of the principal GATT articles.

[25] This thinking is developed in an excellent article on this and related topics by Robert E. Hudec, "The GATT/WTO Dispute Settlement Process: Can it Reconcile Trade Rules and Environment Needs," in Rudiger Wolfrum (ed.), *Enforcing Environmental Standards: Economic Mechanisms as Viable Means*, (Berlin: Springer-Verlag, 1996).

[26] The reasoning in this paragraph draws on Hudec, op. cit. note 25.

[27] For example, tariffs on manufactured imports into industrial countries were reduced from a trade-weighted average of 6.3% to 3.8% as a result of the Uruguay Round. At the time of the establishment of GATT, trade-weighted tariff averages were of the order of 45%. Furthermore, virtually all tariffs in industrial countries were bound, bringing greater stability and predictability to the export markets of developing countries.

[28] See WTO, *Guide to the Uruguay Round Agreements* (Amsterdam, The Netherlands: WTO and Kluwer Law International, 1999), Annex III.

[29] While it is being reasoned here that openness leads to growth, the argument is not being made that the benefits from growth are equitably distributed or that all countries benefit equally from the expanded world income.

[30] The studies also suggest that there will be a significant increase in world trade as a result of the Uruguay Round with estimated increases, depending on type of model used, ranging from 6% to 20%.

[31] See, for example, Sebastian Edwards, "Openness Productivity and Growth: What do we Really Know?" *National Bureau of Economic Research Working Paper*, March 1997; IMF, "Trade as an Engine of Growth," in *World Economic Outlook* (Washington, DC: 1993); and G. Harrison et al., "Quantifying the Uruguay Round," in W. Martin, ed., *The Uruguay Round and the Developing Economies*, Discussion Paper No. 307 (Washington, DC: World Bank, 1995).

[32] In the period 1989–97, the U.S. dollar value of developing countries' exports grew at an annual average rate of 9.7% (as against 7.2% for world merchandise exports) and their imports even faster, by 10.6% per year. The share of developing countries in world trade now stands at 29%. Not all countries have benefitted from the policies described, and the distribution of income has in many instances been far from egalitarian. The share of the 49 least developed countries in world trade (27 of which are WTO members) has fallen from 0.6% to 0.3% over the past decade. The exports of these countries with a combined population of 850 million people is less than half that of Australia. See WTO Secretariat, *Background Document: High Level Symposium on Trade and Development*, Geneva, 17–18 March 1999.

[33] Among the original 23 signatories of the GATT 1947, 11 were developing countries. Currently, more than 100 members of the WTO are developing countries; 29 of these are least-developed countries. Of the 34 countries in various stages of accession to the WTO, all are developing or transition economies.

[34] WTO Secretariat, op. cit. note 32.

[35] See remarks by Renato Ruggerio to the *WTO High Level Symposium on Trade and Environment*, Geneva, 15-16 March 1999.

[36] Like the WTO Agreements, many of the multilateral environmental agreements are intergovernmental in character. The intergovernmental agreements are the focus of this section.

[37] The 1994 GATT consists of the 1947 GATT plus six Understandings that emerged from the Uruguay Round that one way or another refine the original GATT text without changing it.

[38] The second annex sets the rules and procedures for dispute settlement and the third provides for regular reviews of developments in national and international trade policy. The fourth annex relates to four plurilateral trade agreements, only two of which are now in force.

[39] There are exceptions, such as the climate change secretariat.

[40] GATT Secretariat, "Marrakesh Agreement Establishing the World Trade Organization (Article IV)" in *The Results of the Uruguay Round of Multilateral Trade Negotiations: The Legal Texts* (Geneva: GATT Secretariat, 1994).

[41] There are exceptions, as noted earlier. These include the Multifibre Arrangement and the exclusion of agriculture from the normal disciplines of GATT.

[42] This is certainly the conclusion drawn from discussion at a recent symposium conducted by the Institute of Advanced Studies at the United Nations University in collaboration with the Global Environment Information Centre. See the report contained in *Interlinkages: Synergies and Coordination between Multilateral Environment Agreements* (Tokyo: United Nations University, July 1999).

[43] It may meet more frequently if necessary. For example, it met on seven occasions in 1996 to conduct normal business and to prepare the report for the Singapore Ministerial Meeting. It meets informally whenever required.

[44] Some aspects of the work of the committee that are only mentioned here will be addressed in some detail in later chapters.

[45] Article V of the Agreement states that "the General Council may make appropriate arrangements for consultation and cooperation with non-governmental organisations concerned with matters related to those of the WTO."

[46] See *Report (1996) of the Committee on Trade and Environment*, WT/CTE/1, 12 November 1996.

[47] See, for example, Steve Charnovitz, "A Critical Guide to the WTO's Report on Trade and the Environment," *Arizona Journal of International and Comparative Law*, Vol. 14, No. 2 (1997).

CHIEF
CRITICISMS

■ TRANSPARENCY IS OFTEN CALLED A PILLAR of the World Trade Organization (WTO) agreements. In fact, WTO members assign the highest priority to the need for transparency in the conduct of international trade. From a domestic perspective, both the General Agreement on Tariffs and Trade (GATT) and the General Agreement on Trade in Services call for members to publish all measures that affect the operation of the agreements. Members are also required to notify all other members of any general laws and regulations on WTO matters. Some agreements have their own specific notification requirements, and some require the establishment of inquiry points to ensure access to information on domestic regulations. The Sanitary and Phytosanitary Agreement and the Technical Barriers to Trade Agreement require members to notify each other if new local standards affecting trade deviate from international standards. Members review the trade policies of other countries carefully. The only trade restriction legally permitted on a general basis in the WTO is the tariff, in good part because of its transparency.

Despite all these rules and requirements about information exchange, the WTO is frequently perceived as a nontransparent organization. This perception is not new. The 1985 report of the Leutwiler Group of Eminent Persons, which convened in the GATT to address systemic issues prior to the launching of the Uruguay Round, remarked that a "major reason why things have gone wrong with the trading system is that trade policy actions have often escaped scrutiny and discussion at the national level. Clearer analysis and greater openness in the making of trade policy are badly needed, along with greater public knowledge of how the multilateral system works."[1]

Fifteen years later, the WTO is bitterly criticized for its lack of transparency. Nowhere was this more apparent than in the Seattle demonstrations. One problem is the difficulty in obtaining information on activities of the organization itself. If it is hard to find out what the WTO is doing, the critics say, the organization must have something to hide.[2] In this respect, there are two key questions. Is there a lack of information on WTO activities?

If so, what would be the disadvantages for the WTO—if any—of making more information available?

The criticism also extends to the perception that the WTO is not accountable—or even responsive—to the needs and concerns of non-governmental organizations (NGOs). Their representatives, for example, are not permitted to be present in even the least important WTO meetings. Here, too, there are a number of important questions. Should NGOs be present or represented at WTO meetings? If so, would this affect the intergovernmental character of the organization? If there is a feeling of exclusion, isn't it up to WTO members to develop an effective communications strategy and to establish, at the domestic level, broad consultative processes with organizations of civil society, in order to give them the opportunity to weigh in on the process of trade policy formulation? Is there a role for action at the multilateral level to complement national efforts?

Transparency and the need for public support for the WTO generally have taken on increased importance as a result of the Seattle meeting. These issues have been discussed in the WTO under three broad headings:

- raising the general level of awareness about the WTO;

- establishing formal avenues of cooperation with NGOs and intergovernmental organizations; and

- accelerating the process of "derestricting" documents so that they become available more quickly to interested parties.

Each of these will be discussed in turn. The general approach adopted here is that it is in the interests of the WTO to become far more transparent in its activities than the GATT was. The organization has little to hide. All the rules and procedures are in the public domain, and while the application of some of these rules may not please everyone, there is no reason to delay publication of documents that will eventually enter the public domain. In fact, the only documents that should be restricted are those that require confidentiality to protect national interests; very few documents fall into this category. The restricted nature of some WTO documents makes it harder for WTO members to explain clearly to domestic constituencies the rationale for national policies toward the WTO.

KNOWLEDGE OF THE WTO
AND ITS ACTIVITIES

■ IN THE VIEW OF WTO MEMBERS, IT IS UP TO national governments to inform the public of the role and activities of the WTO, as they do for other multilateral institutions. Notwithstanding, there has been considerable pressure for the WTO Secretariat to fill a gap created by a failure of many governments to inform the public about WTO activities. The Secretariat has responded with a number of initiatives. In fact, recent experience shows that much can and has been done to increase awareness of the activities of the WTO. The creation of the WTO Web site was an important initiative, and one apparently much appreciated. Individual users rose to 200,000 during October 1999, a 60-percent increase since January 1999.[3] Visitors to the site most often consult the links that provide access to WTO documents.

In addition, the WTO Secretariat has organized joint symposia involving WTO members, representatives of intergovernmental organizations, and environmental NGOs to discuss some of the most controversial issues in the trade and environmental debate. Representatives of well over 100 NGOs have been joined at recent meetings by delegations from the majority of WTO members. The most recent symposium, in March 1999, involved ministers, heads of international organizations, and senior officials or heads of NGOs.

In an effort to raise the awareness of officials in developing countries about trade and environmental issues and how they are dealt with in the Committee on Trade and Environment (CTE), the WTO Secretariat organized seven regional seminars in developing and central European countries in 1998. These involved officials from trade ministries as well as environment ministries. A key objective of these meetings was to improve national coordination in an area where it is clearly important. WTO members themselves have pointed out this need on many occasions.[4]

Although coordination among officials in various parts of governments is a responsibility at the national level, these seminars revealed that the meetings were the first occasion when some trade and environmental officials from the same country had actually met. The gatherings evolved to the point where three days of meetings of government officials were immediately followed by an additional two days with regional NGO representatives (whose participation was organized by the International Centre for Trade and Sustainable Development in Geneva). For such meetings to be effective, experience has shown that they should be followed up by further contact with the participating officials.

. . . .

WTO RELATIONS WITH OTHER GROUPS AND INSTITUTIONS

■ CRITICISM OF THE WTO WITH RESPECT TO transparency includes the charge that the WTO is neither accountable nor responsive to the needs and concerns of society at large. It has been argued that the participation of NGO representatives in various WTO activities would only enrich WTO deliberations because of their experience and expertise in a number of the areas under discussion. The counter-argument, once again, is that it is the role of national governments to keep all parts of society fully informed of developments of interest to them in intergovernmental bodies and to take the public's concerns into account as appropriate.

NONGOVERNMENTAL ORGANIZATIONS

In August 1948 in Geneva, the head of the GATT presented a set of recommendations on the organization's relations with NGOs.[5] He proposed that a list of NGOs with consultative status be drawn up. Representatives of these groups would be invited to send observers to the annual meetings of the GATT. They would receive documentation and be invited to propose items for the conference agenda. The Director-General (then called the Executive Director) would consult with NGOs with special competence in a particular subject area if there were specific proposals entrusted to the Director-General or any of the subsidiary bodies of the organization. On general matters, the Director-General would have the authority to establish an Advisory Committee of NGOs. The listed NGOs would receive copies of all derestricted documentation, and documents submitted by NGOs would be distributed at the discretion of the Director-General. The Director-General would circulate a list of all communications from listed NGOs, and any of the documents could have full distribution if so requested by a member. Fifty years later, many elements of this earlier proposal are again under review.

According to the Agreement Establishing the WTO (Article V.2), the "General Council may make appropriate arrangements for consultation and co-operation with non-governmental organizations with matters related to those of the WTO."[6] In July 1996, the General Council adopted *WTO Guidelines for Arrangements on Relations with Non-Governmental Organizations*. A further statement of intention emerged during the May 1998 Ministerial Meeting in Geneva, when WTO members "recognized the importance of enhancing public understanding of the benefits of the multilateral trading system in order to build support for it and agree to work towards this end. In this context we will consider how to improve the transparency of WTO operations." For its part, the CTE is mandated to "provide input to the relevant bodies in respect of appropriate arrangements for relations with inter-governmental organizations referred to in Article V of the WTO."[7]

The guidelines adopted by the General Council in 1996 recognize the role that NGOs can play in increasing public awareness of the WTO and the need for increasing the transparency of WTO operations. They mention specifically the need to make documents available more readily than in the past. The guidelines mandate the Secretariat to play a more active role in its direct contacts with NGOs and recommend the development of a number of ways to interact with NGOs, including symposia on specific WTO-related issues. They also envision the possibility of the chairpersons of WTO councils and committees participating in discussions or meetings with NGOs, although only in their personal capacity. The guidelines do state that there is currently a "broadly held view that it would not be possible for NGOs to be directly involved in the work of the WTO or its meetings." They also note that the WTO is a legally binding treaty of rights and obligations among its members and a forum for negotiations, and that the primary responsibility for taking into account the different elements of public interest lies at the national level.

Based on these guidelines, a number of steps have been taken by the WTO Secretariat to increase its interaction with NGOs. These extend beyond the holding of the symposia described earlier, a process that had its origins prior to the guidelines but that received a considerable boost from their adoption. The Director-General proposed at the meeting of the General

Council on 15–16 July 1998 that the Secretariat hold regular briefings for NGOs and compile a monthly list of documents received from NGOs to be circulated to all members.[8] An NGO forum has also been created on the WTO Web site. In the view of most members, however, closer consultation and cooperation with NGOs should occur at the national level, where the principal effort should be made to take into account the different elements of public interest in trade policy.

Transparency is also a priority of the work of the Organisation for Economic Co-operation and Development (OECD) on trade and environmental issues. In 1993, for example, the Joint Working Party on Trade and Environment adopted procedural guidelines to encourage transparency and consultation with civil society, the review of trade and environmental policies and agreements from the perspective of other policy arenas, international cooperation in environmental action, and the involvement of all stakeholders in solving trade and environmental disputes.[9] The OECD working party subsequently agreed to identify "activities and mechanisms which have been put in place by governments and governmental agencies to promote transparency and public participation" on trade and environment issues.[10] A number of case studies have been prepared by the OECD secretariat describing the experience of government and civil society representatives with the practice of transparency and consultation.[11] The Joint Working Party eventually plans to consider identifying good practices in transparency and consultation.

Although the results of these studies may prove otherwise, work to date indicates that governments have been far from effective in building mechanisms to consult with NGOs on trade matters. In a survey of 30 countries, one study revealed that formal mechanisms for consultation with NGOs are rare.[12] In fact, only three governments effectively involved NGOs at the national level in WTO work. Governments may agree that the primary responsibility for interacting with NGOs lies at the national level, but it may well be their failure to fulfill their own objectives in this area that has contributed to greater pressure being placed on the multilateral process to inform and involve NGOs.

Against this backdrop, an important question is whether there are initiatives at the multilateral level that would support improved national processes. There is little doubt that the WTO should contribute to greater openness through a comprehensive policy of increased access to information, as discussed later in the section on derestriction of documents. Greater and more systematic use of opportunities for consultation with organizations of civil society at the multilateral level should also complement the dialogue at the domestic level. The guidelines adopted by the General Council in July 1996 entrust the Secretariat with organizing various ways to interact with NGOs, such as symposia. However, no budgetary arrangements have been made for these initiatives.

One frequently made proposal is that NGOs should participate in some manner in WTO meetings to improve their appreciation of the process. NGO advocates argue that their direct involvement would enrich the functioning of the WTO.[13] The thrust of these proposals is not that NGOs should have a role in the process of intergovernmental negotiation. That, it is invariably acknowledged, is something for governments alone.

The view of the significant majority of WTO members is that it would be inappropriate to allow NGOs to participate directly even as observers in the proceedings of WTO meetings, including the CTE. One concern of WTO members, as elaborated in Chapter 2, is that the special character of the WTO as both a legally binding instrument and a forum for negotiations requires that it remain strictly intergovernmental. WTO members also argue that if NGOs are concerned about a lack of information (for example, about committee proceedings), this strengthens the case for more rapid derestriction of summary records of meetings, but not for participation in the meetings themselves.

But it should be underscored that the participation of NGOs in negotiations is indeed an option. If a government wants to have an NGO—or any other representative of an interest group—present at a particular meeting, that option is already available. Indeed, a number of governments had nongovernmental representation on their delegations at the Seattle meeting. In the past, however, most governments have resisted requests for nongovernmental representation—a pressure with which they are quite familiar. Business lobbyists frequently try to exercise their influence directly by getting appointed to a national delegation. For this reason, to lessen domestic pressure, it is perhaps convenient at the national level for a government to say that participation in WTO meetings is not permitted. But governments are indeed free to include whomever they choose in their national delegations.

Even if there were a desire on the part of all WTO members to admit NGOs to WTO working meetings as observers, it would not be easy to implement that goal in practice. The criteria for the admission of NGOs are not at all clear. Should, for example, representatives of nonprofit industry and labor confederation groups be admitted as NGOs?

Opening the door of the WTO to the participation of NGOs raises several other practical concerns. Which groups of civil society should be represented at different meetings, and who would decide? Is the size of the NGO or whether it represents a large part of society an important consideration? Should farmers' unions be present during negotiations on the reduction of agricultural subsidies that lead to environmental degradation, or should environmental NGOs? Should consumer groups be present during negotiations when trade liberalization leading to lower consumer prices was being discussed, or should it be the sectoral interests that would be adversely affected by a lowering of trade barriers? Who should be present during talks about restricting trade in products derived from genetically modified organisms? Is it not preferable to have a democratically elected government represent the diverse interest groups in a given country?

It is useful for the Director-General to meet from time to time with NGOs, and for the Secretariat to hold briefing sessions, but it is much more important for NGOs to have access to their governments. The important issue here is whether there should be some institutionalized arrangement. A number of proposals have been forthcoming in this respect from NGOs— some of them carefully prepared and convincingly argued.[14] I revisit these proposals in the final chapter of this volume.

INTERGOVERNMENTAL ORGANIZATIONS

In July 1996, the General Council also adopted *Guidelines for Observer Status for International Intergovernmental Organizations in the WTO*. The CTE agreed to extend observer status on a permanent basis to the intergovernmental organizations that previously participated as observers on an ad hoc basis and has subsequently included additional organizations on this list. Currently 23 intergovernmental organizations sit in as observers at the CTE.

Observer status for secretariats of relevant multilateral environmental agreements (MEAs) can play a positive role in creating a clearer appreciation of the mutually supportive role of trade and environmental policies and in identifying areas of potential conflict before they become a serious problem. For example, it is widely accepted that it is useful for MEA representatives to brief the CTE on the use of trade measures applied pursuant to the MEAs. This gives the CTE a chance to express its view to MEA authorities on trade measures being considered under an MEA. Consultation and cooperation between the secretariats of the WTO and MEAs are also useful, especially during initial negotiations and amendments of MEAs.

A further example of productive intergovernmental information sharing has been the initiative of WTO members to invite to the CTE representatives of the secretariats of relevant MEAs. WTO members have been directly informed of the objectives and workings of the MEAs and the implications—if any—for the WTO. During the June 1999 meeting of the CTE, the secretariats of seven MEAs were invited to send representatives.[15]

. . . .

ACCESS TO DOCUMENTS

■ THE GENERAL COUNCIL ADOPTED *Procedures for the Circulation and Derestriction of WTO Documents* in July 1996 as well. WTO members agreed in principle that all documents should be circulated as unrestricted. Although this principle is subject to exceptions specified in an appendix, any document containing public information must be circulated as unrestricted, and any member is free to order any of its submissions circulated as unrestricted. Furthermore, any document may be considered for derestriction at any time.[16]

Restricted documents are generally derestricted six months after circulation to governments. The July 1996 decision provided for the General Council to review, and if necessary modify, these derestriction procedures two years after their adoption. In July 1998, members started the process of devising more transparent WTO procedures, including earlier derestriction of documents (primarily ones listed in the appendix).[17]

The WTO has managed to increase substantially the availability of documents to the public. Nevertheless, even though the WTO is a far more transparent organization than the GATT was, the current derestriction procedures still have a number of shortcomings. Delay in derestriction seriously limits the value of documents for public information. There appears to be no clear justification for a rule that makes documents available to the public only after an artificial deadline. The restricted nature of some WTO documents makes it harder for WTO members to explain clearly to domestic constituencies the rationale for national activities regarding the WTO. In addition, requests for early derestriction can result in a selective and partial release of information, which has on occasion provoked unnecessary controversy among WTO members. A general rule under which most types of WTO documents would be immediately derestricted would avoid the risk of selectivity and ensure an fuller accounting of WTO activities.

. . . .

THE DISPUTE SETTLEMENT PROCESS

■ AS FAR AS THE DISPUTE SETTLEMENT PROCESS is concerned, it would seem that there are at least four issues of relevance with respect to WTO transparency: 1) submissions of amicus briefs by NGOs, 2) public circulation of panel submissions by parties to a dispute at the time they are submitted to the panels, 3) public access to panel hearings, and 4) circulation of panel reports. The first three topics are taken up in Chapter 7, in which I look at the dispute-settlement system in greater detail.

With respect to the circulation of dispute panel reports, it has been argued that the reports are published too long after panels have completed their work. Reports are actually circulated to governments and the public at the same time, although this can, indeed, occur some time after a panel has completed its work. This is largely due to practical considerations relating to the processing of documentation. Given the length of the reports, reproduction and distribution takes time. The shrimp-turtle panel report, for example, which the NGO community was eager to review, ran to 431 single-spaced pages. The length of panel reports is, in turn, a function of the fact that members insist on the publication of the secretariat summaries of the argumentation of the cases alongside the panel findings. In the view of the members, these summaries provide evidence that the case has been comprehensively argued. This of course is not unrelated to the lack of transparency in the process, as discussed in Chapter 7. Distribution is further delayed by the requirement that reports be circulated only when they are available in all three working languages of the WTO. They can then be read by officials everywhere at the same time and reacted to accordingly.

NOTES

[1] See the Leutwiler Report, *Trade Policies for a Better Future: Proposals for Action* (Geneva: GATT Secretariat, 1985).

[2] One conclusion drawn by some is that the nontransparent character has unnecessarily raised suspicions about the WTO leading to a loss of public support. At their annual summit held in Cologne 18–20 June 1999, the G8 leaders confirmed their agreement on "the importance of improving the WTO's transparency and of making it more responsive to civil society while preserving its intergovernmental nature."

[3] The WTO home page is accessible at <http://www.wto.org>.

[4] Achieving the "joint objectives of WTO member governments in the areas of trade, environment and sustainable development requires policy coordination at the national level." See WTO, *Report of the Committee on Trade and Environment*, WT/CTE/1, 12 November 1996, para 168.

[5] Additional detail on the early history GATT-NGO relations can be found in a most useful publication on matters of interest to NGOs and WTO officials. See International Centre for Trade and Sustainable Development, *Bridges Between Trade and Sustainable Development* (Geneva: ICTSD, June 1998).

[6] GATT Secretariat, *Results of the Uruguay Round of Multilateral Trade Negotiations: The Legal Texts* (Geneva: GATT Secretariat, 1994).

[7] See WTO, *Report of the Committee on Trade and Environment*, WT/CTE/1, 12 November 1996, paras 212–218.

[8] The details for NGO participation in Ministerial Meetings etc. can be found in Gabriella Marceau and Peter N. Pedersen, "Is the WTO Open and Transparent—A Discussion of the Relationship of the WTO with Non-Governmental Organisations and Civil Society's Claim for More Transparency and Public Participation," *Journal of World Trade*, Vol. 33, No. 1 (February 1999). This paper also addresses in some detail the briefing sessions provided for NGOs by the Secretariat.

[9] See Organisation for Economic Co-operation and Development (OECD), *Report on Trade and Environment*, Council at Ministerial Level, 26–27 May, C/MIN(99)14, 12 May 1999.

[10] See OECD, *Transparency and Consultation on Trade and Environment*, Joint Working Party on Trade and Environment, COM/TD/ENV(99)26, 30 March 1999.

[11] The countries and organizations studied are Australia, Canada, the European Union, France, Germany, Netherlands, United Kingdom, and the United States.

[12] See Christophe Bellmann and Richard Gerster, "Accountability in the World Trade Organization," *Journal of World Trade*, Vol. 30, No. 6 (December 1996).

[13] See, for example, Daniel C. Esty, "Environmental Governance at the WTO," in Gary P. Sampson and W. Bradnee Chambers (eds.), *Trade, Environment and the Millennium* (Tokyo: United Nations University Press, 1999), and Bellmann and Gerster, op. cit. note 13.

[14] See, for example, International Institute for Sustainable Development, *Six Easy Pieces: Five Things the WTO Should Do—And One It Should Not*, presented to WTO High Level Symposium on Trade and the Environment, Geneva, 16–17 March 1999, mimeo.

[15] These were CITES, the Montreal Protocol, the Climate Change Convention, the Intergovernmental Forum on Forests, and the International Tropical Timber Organization. The Convention on Biological Diversity and the Convention of Antarctic Living Resources did not attend but did make written submissions.

[16] For example, CTE documents that were considered relevant for the 1998 Symposium were derestricted well in advance of the normal date to ensure their availability.

[17] These documents include draft agendas, draft decisions and proposals, working papers, confidential documents relating to negotiating positions, minutes of meetings, documents relating to the accession of future WTO members, reports on balance-of-payments consultations, and panel reports that are derestricted within 10 days after their circulation to members.

WIN-WIN SCENARIOS

■ WHEN CONFRONTED WITH THE CRITICISM THAT TRADE is bad for the environment, the trade community generally points out that it is inappropriate resource usage and consumption patterns—not trade per se—that damages the environment. In fact, when adverse production and consumption externalities are adequately integrated into decision-making processes, trade liberalization and the attainment of environmental objectives can be mutually supportive.[1] Trade liberalization leads to a more efficient use of resources; a more efficient relative price structure (trade restrictions themselves are market distortions); more resources available for environmental management programs because of growth in real income; and an increase in the availability of environment-related goods and services through market liberalization. Not surprisingly, an important issue within the context of the World Trade Organization (WTO) has been the examination of ways in which this positive link between trade liberalization and improvement of the environment can be exploited.[2]

To take advantage of this link, the ministers directed the Committee on Trade and Environment (CTE) to study the environmental benefits of removing trade restrictions and distortions.[3] In the jargon of the CTE, members have been exploring the possibilities of trade liberalization in industrial countries where "win-win" scenarios exist. Industrial countries win when they remove trade restrictions that are environmentally harmful in their own countries; developing countries win when exports grow following the removal of environmentally harmful trade restrictions in the importing countries.

And, there is, in fact, a third win. Numerous empirical studies have demonstrated that the link between trade liberalization and economic growth is unequivocal. As noted in Chapter 2, countries that have opted for an outward-oriented development strategy have been the fastest growing in the developing world. Higher gross domestic product per capita and fewer resources used to produce each unit of output mean a higher national income and more resources available for the implementation of sound environmental policies. This does not mean, however, that the link between growth and liberalization cannot be challenged. Economic growth may lead to more wealth but does not in itself ensure an egalitarian society. Nor does it mean that growth will automatically lead to an improvement in the environment. Other complementary policies may well be required.

At the moment, there is clearly an environmental problem to respond to in terms of inefficient government intervention in the marketplace. The Report of the High Level Advisory Group on the Environment to the Secretary-General of the Organisation for Economic Co-operation and Development (OECD) noted that government interventions are frequently "economically perverse, ecologically destructive and trade distorting, sometimes all at the same time. The OECD has a crucial leadership role to play in . . . proposing policy reforms that would ensure that market forces can work both for the environment and the economy simultaneously and not one at the expense of another."[4]

There are many good reasons for promoting a win-win approach. It would give force to the commitment of WTO members to use the world's resources optimally and in accordance with the objective of sustainable development. It would provide evidence of their desire to protect and preserve the environment and to enhance the means for doing so precisely when they are being criticized for not doing enough.[5] Viewed constructively, by adopting a win-win approach, public support can be garnered for undertaking reform in sectors where some interest groups may be adversely affected by policy reform, but where reform is in the interests of the community at large (see Chapter 2). The initiative is already viewed positively by some environmental nongovernmental organizations (NGOs) that have been hostile to the WTO in other areas. In addition, the agenda item of trade liberalization holds attraction for developing countries where few other advantages are seen in the trade and environmental debate.

At the insistence of developing countries, the discussion in the CTE on this agenda item is limited to environmental advantages associated with the removal of trade restrictions in industrial countries. It does not extend to the possibility of environmental degradation in developing countries through trade expansion.[6] As noted in Chapter 2, developing countries have resisted creating a link whereby their improved market access is contingent on meeting predetermined standards or adopting certain policies domestically, be they related to the environment, labor conditions, or anything else.

One important question is whether win-win situations do in fact exist. The answer is that they do—in principle. From a trade perspective, different environmental resource endowments (such as the physical capacity to absorb pollution) are themselves a basis for differences in true comparative advantage. Furthermore, different societies and individuals within them also have different levels of tolerance with respect to environmental degradation. As long as national sovereignty prevails with respect to environmental priorities, the extent to which externalities are internalized will be determined by awareness of the environmental problem, the government's capacity to adopt the necessary policy measure to deal with it, the nation's physical capacity to absorb the environmental damage, and societal preferences relating to environmental conditions and the quality of life. This in turn will influence the impact on relative prices nationally and internationally. Trade restrictions can distort the optimal functioning of markets, and thus the exploitation of comparative advantage, just as they can frustrate the implementation of sound environmental management policies.

Discussion in the CTE has revealed that win-win situations exist in practice as well as in principle. A number of priority sectors for further work were identified and listed in the report of the CTE to the Singapore ministerial meeting.[7] Through discussion of national submissions and Secretariat documentation, the CTE identified the most prevalent trade restrictions and distortions in various sectors—agriculture, energy, fisheries, forestry products, natural-resource-based products, nonferrous metals, textiles and clothing, leather, and environmental services—along with the environmental benefits associated with their removal.

Periodically there have been calls for a multilateral framework to facilitate the assessment of the environmental impact of trade liberalization on the environment.[8] The view has been that there is a need for WTO members to think more comprehensively about a trade agenda that is supportive of sustainable development. Although governments can proceed domestically and in other fora to address the harmful environmental effects, work should also proceed to take advantage of the potential environmental benefits of trade liberalization. After making a proposal for a multilateral framework in 1994, the Commission on Sustainable Development was mandated by governments to provide the institutional coordination necessary to assess the environmental and social development aspects of trade policies. At the WTO High Level Symposium on Trade and Environment, the United States announced that like the European Union, Canada, and Norway, it would carry out an assessment of the likely environmental implications of the post-2000 WTO negotiations.

There has been some discussion of the possibility of all members agreeing to carry out such environmental impact assessment studies under

WTO auspices, but the idea has not gained broad-based support. For most countries, the decision of whether to conduct such studies is a national choice that has little to do with the work of the WTO. The potential for building public support, however, by exploring how to avoid or ease any adverse effects on the environment following trade liberalization seems clear. In this respect, useful work is proceeding in various international organizations, governments, academic institutions, and NGOs.[9]

. . . .

PRIORITY SECTORS

■ THE TASK OF EVALUATING ENVIRONMENTAL BENEFITS to be derived from removing trade restrictions and distortions in all WTO members is complicated not only by the complexity of the changes in the resource usage and consumption patterns that follow trade liberalization and the concomitant changes in relative prices, but also by the limited capacity to measure environmental impact in many countries.[10] Work has proceeded in the CTE, however, with a narrower focus on identifying sectors where environmental benefits follow trade liberalization.[11] Notwithstanding the complexities of the task, a number of conclusions can be drawn that allow priorities to be assigned to various sectors.[12]

FISHERIES

In the case of fisheries, a sector of considerable importance to developing countries, the link between depleted fish stocks and bad government policy seems to be well accepted.[13] Fisheries subsidies are widespread, and they distort trade and undermine the sustainable use of the resource base.[14] One reason for giving priority to this sector is that useful substantive work has already been done in the WTO and elsewhere, and there is evidence that the political will to address the problem appears to be strengthening. Indeed, for many environmentalists, one of the chief disappointments of the collapse of the Seattle Ministerial was that it stranded a proposal to initiate WTO negotiations on reductions in fishery subsidies, which appeared to be gaining broad international support.

Both New Zealand[15] and the United States[16] had submitted proposals to the CTE on the environmental benefits of removing subsidies in this sector. Australia, Iceland, New Zealand, the Philippines, and the United States issued a joint declaration at the 1999 WTO High Level Symposium on Trade and the Environment to "highlight the beneficial contribution that the elimination of environmentally damaging and trade distorting subsidization of the fisheries sector would make to the conservation and sustainable use of fish stocks and the promotion of sustainable development."[17] A number of countries had formally assigned a priority to the removal of these subsidies at the meeting in Seattle, and specific proposals on how to proceed had been made.[18] The World Wide Fund for Nature (WWF) has explored the extent of fishing subsidies and the degree to which those by WTO members breach their obligations.[19] The WTO Secretariat has also detailed the relevant disciplines that exist in the WTO Subsidy Agreement, and listed subsidies in this sector at the national level that have been notified to the WTO in accordance with the requirements of the agreement.[20] (Many other non-notified subsidies do, of course, exist in WTO member countries.)

In addition, several symposia have raised awareness of the need for reform in this sector, citing subsidies as a major source of fish stock depletion. The U.N. Conference on Trade and Development, the U.N. Environment Programme, and WWF were jointly responsible for a Fisheries Symposium that addressed among other things the impact on individual fish species of a failure of government policies.[21] In this exercise, offending countries and products were identified.

AGRICULTURE

Agriculture could also be considered a priority sector and of considerable interest to developing countries.[22] The Chairman's Summary of the G15 Ministerial Conference in Bangalore, India, in August 1999 states that to "show the mutual supportiveness of trade and environment, trade distortive agricultural export subsidies should be removed by developed countries." Unfortunately, there could be no agreement to do so at the Seattle meeting. Even those who defend intervention in this sector do not deny the link between market distortions and environmental degradation, given the many well-known examples of externalities not being reflected in market prices. More work has been done on the environmental damage associated with government intervention here than in any other sector, and the results show an unequivocal relationship between the direct, negative, and often significant environmental effects stemming from market access restrictions, domestic support policies, and export subsidies.

According to discussion in the CTE, agricultural subsidies have led to intensified land use, increased applications of agrochemicals, adoption of intensive animal production practices and overgrazing, degradation of natural resources, loss of natural wildlife habitats and biodiversity, reduced agricultural diversity, and expansion of agricultural production into marginal and ecologically sensitive areas.[23] Agricultural assistance through output-related policies in many industrial countries has imposed high environmental costs on other nations that have a comparative advantage in agricultural production and trade.[24]

There is, however, a clear development dimension in agricultural trade liberalization. First, there are direct links. Many developing countries have an export capacity in agricultural products. If market access restrictions are removed, their exports will increase. Second, quantitative studies reveal that government interventions through trade-related measures in this sector depress world agricultural prices so that poor farmers stay poor. And low prices and rural poverty induce these farmers to cultivate marginal lands subject to erosion and runoff and to clear forests for agricultural extension.

Yet the removal of trade restrictions and distortions in agricultural trade must coincide with the respect of other WTO commitments. More specifically, the least developed and the net food-importing developing countries have stressed that they would suffer from the higher world prices flowing from the removal of government intervention in this sector. Action with respect to the WTO Marrakesh Ministerial Decision providing for guidelines to ensure that an increasing proportion of basic foodstuff aid is given in the form of grants, or on appropriate concessional terms, would have to accompany the removal of agricultural trade restrictions and distortions.[25]

Attempts by developing country governments to offset low prices by providing input subsidies for fertilizers and pesticides produce much the same results of soil erosion and intensive chemical use as in highly protected agricultural markets, but they also involve greater threats to the health of local farmers and consumers from the incorrect application of agrochemicals.[26] In fact, the removal of trade restrictions in the agricultural sector could well touch on some of the most impoverished developing countries, many of which benefitted little from the tariff reductions and preferences accorded to manufactured goods.[27]

Another practical consideration in assigning priority to the agriculture sector is that there is the possibility in the medium term for the negotiated reduction of trade restrictions and distortions. Even in the absence of agreement in Seattle, negotiations aimed at further liberalizing agricultural trade are set to begin in 2000, as required by the 1994 Agreement on Agriculture. Knowledge of the environmental damage that can arise from certain trade restrictions should increase popular support for further liberalization in this sector.

FOREST PRODUCTS

The treatment of forest products goes hand in hand with the agricultural sector, as the removal of support to the latter can reduce pressure for agricultural extension into ecologically marginal land, including forest areas. Many types of measures are known to affect trade in this sector, including tariffs and tariff escalation, subsidies, export taxes and restrictions, certification of sustainable forest management and labeling of forest products, market transparency for forest products, promotion of less-used forest species, and financing and technology to improve sustainable forest management and increase value-added processing of wood and wood products. Some measures have positive effects on the environment.

Of these measures, tariff escalation is believed to be the main source of trade restriction and distortion in this sector. It can change production patterns and have a second-round negative effect on developing countries. Export taxes and other restrictions on unprocessed timber exports are used by some timber-exporting countries to encourage forest-based industrialization. These are reinforced by other measures giving preferential treatment to domestic processing industries, such as supplying raw materials to local producers at below world market prices, with an inefficient use of raw materials as a result. In certain cases they are used to compensate domestic processors for tariff escalation and other market access barriers faced in major export markets.[28]

Establishing appropriate production and consumption patterns in forests is important for other reasons in addition to the revenue associated with logging. Forests are important, for example, in soil-fixing, carbon sequestration, and economic and noneconomic considerations relating to biodiversity. Thus the concerns relating to forestry management on the part of governments are broadening to encompass integrated land use issues. One result is that a variety of direct and indirect subsidies are now applied in the forestry sector that have considerable implications for the management of forestry resources and eventually trade.[29]

It was evident in Seattle, however, that some groups do not see forest products as a win-win opportunity. Based on an initiative that originated in discussions within the context of the Asia-Pacific Economic Cooperation forum, negotiations on the accelerated liberalization of a number of traded products were proposed at Seattle.[30] Nine sectors had been identified as liberalization priorities, including forest products (and fisheries). This provoked a strong reaction from a number of environmental groups, which saw few if any benefits from trade liberalization in this sector. These groups argued that expanded trade in forest products would lead to unsustainable logging rates and the spread of invasive pests.[31] While a case can certainly be made for not trading a product if it leads to unacceptable environmental degradation, it would appear that in the case of both of these objections, the source of the problem lies not with trade, per se, but with inadequate policies outside the area of trade policy.

ENERGY

Energy could also be a priority sector, because unlike some other sectors, production is not an end in itself; energy is an important input to almost all economic activities. Reforming energy policies will affect virtually every aspect of economic activity. By distorting prices, energy subsidies exacerbate environmental problems linked to energy production and use. For example, some subsidies may encourage the inefficient use of energy resources, discourage energy conservation, or constrain the expanded use of renewable sources. In addition, subsidies may encourage obsolete and environmentally inefficient technologies to continue operation. Another reason for assigning a priority to this sector is that a vast amount of work is being undertaken in connection with the Framework Convention on Climate Change and its subsequent protocols. As discussed in Chapter 6, market-based policy reform is identified as an objective of the Kyoto Protocol. Much of the information gathered for these purposes could be utilized.

Governments identified specific products in this sector as priorities for negotiations; Brazil has presented a formal submission to the CTE spelling out why trade liberalization in ethanol products is a win-win situation.[32]

ENVIRONMENTAL GOODS AND SERVICES

A final sector where liberalization could be beneficial for all is trade in environmental goods and services (pollution control, for example, or solid waste management). The value of world production in this sector is considerable and has been estimated to be in the order of $450 billion a year.[33] In this sector, as in others, it is in the interest of all WTO members that environmentally sound goods and services be made available on the international market at the cheapest prevailing world prices.[34] After studying liberalization in this sector, the OECD Report to the Council of Ministers concluded that goods and services would become cheaper, meaning that "limited environmental protection budgets can be stretched further" and that "expanded market opportunities can encourage technological progress, as well as providing economies of scale and increased efficiency."[35]

Buying goods and services at world market prices is of course an option available to all countries, as governments can unilaterally remove barriers to imports in these goods and services and so serve their own interests. In practice, however, governments seek "concessions" in negotiations even when acting in their own interests, and the possibility of obtaining such concessions is greatest in multilateral rounds of negotiations where the removal of barriers to imports in one sector can traded for liberalization in another. In recent years, however, traditional cross-sectoral trade-offs have not always been necessary to encourage governments to enter into sectoral trade-liberalizing negotiations. Reaping the advantages that ensue from trade liberalization and a more efficient resource use on both the consumption and production side has been the driving force in a variety of sectors; examples include information technology, pharmaceutical products, basic telecommunications, and financial services. Should not such sectoral negotiations extend to environmental goods and services?

In many other sectors, of course, the removal of trade restrictions and distortions will also lead to a win-win scenario. Included in this category are ferrous and nonferrous metals, leather products, textiles, and clothing. Thus products in these sectors should certainly not be excluded from a list of potential candidates for accelerated liberalization on the grounds of environmental improvement.

SOME CAVEATS

There are several caveats to the foregoing discussion. First, the CTE's work has been confined to examining the positive effects of trade liberalization on the environment in industrial countries. As noted earlier, the possible negative effects of trade expansion on developing countries have not been on the agenda. In reality, negative links between trade liberalization and the environment certainly exist. Without the appropriate policies in place, trade can push resource usage to unsustainable rates, and even with the growth that can come from expanded trade, there is no guarantee that the newly created resources will be used for environmental management programs. But as frequently noted, the WTO is in the business of promoting growth through expanded trade—not, according to its current terms of reference, of implementing or evaluating the effectiveness of environmental management policies in individual countries. Trade liberalization needs to be accompanied by sound environmental management policies.

A second caveat relates to the emphasis given to environmentally unfriendly subsidies.[36] There are, however, numerous other trade distortions that damage the environment and lead to overproduction. In the case of agriculture, for example, tariffs remain high, and although the Uruguay Round agreements curtailed the use of nontariff measures, these remain widespread. Restrictive import licensing is used in conjunction with minimum access obligations; some variable agricultural tariffs and production and export subsidies remain, as do export taxes and quotas designed to ensure low-cost supply for domestic consumers. State trading activities that may distort prices continue despite privatization programs.

Finally, not all trade-related measures adversely affect the environment. Indeed, subsidies used to encourage the use of environmentally friendly technology provide an example. Some such subsidies are allowed as exemptions from the rules restricting subsidies in the WTO Agreement on Subsidies. Other examples include measures that correct for excessive resource use as part of a well-constructed environmental management policy. The intention of the win-win initiative is clearly not to question those measures that have as their objective the improvement of the environment and that do not unnecessarily restrict international trade.

NOTES

[1] For a discussion of the process of "internalizing the externalities," see Dan Esty, *Greening the GATT* (Washington, DC: International Institute for Economics, July 1994).

[2] For a comprehensive discussion see World Trade Organization (WTO), *Trade and Environment*, Special Studies 4 (Geneva: October 1999).

[3] See Marrakesh Ministerial Decision on Trade and Environment, April 1994.

[4] Organisation for Economic Co-operation and Development (OECD), *Report of the High Level Advisory Group in the Environment to the Secretary General of the OECD*, TD/TC(98)3, 16 February 1988, p. 22.

[5] See the Preamble to the *Agreement Establishing the World Trade Organization*.

[6] For a discussion in the context of sustainable development, see the Australian Submission to the Committee on Trade and Environment (CTE), *Trade Liberalisation, the Environment and Sustainable Development*, WT/CTE/W36, 23 June 1996.

[7] The sectors for further work are specified in paragraph 198 of WTO, *Report of the Committee on Trade and Environment to Ministers of Singapore*, WT/CTE/1 (Geneva: WTO, 12 November 1996).

[8] See, for example, World Wide Fund for Nature International, *Initiating an Environmental Assessment of Trade Liberalisation in the WTO*, WWF Discussion paper (Gland, Switzerland: WWF, March 1999).

[9] See, for example, the papers submitted to the OECD Workshop on Methodologies for Environmental Assessment of Trade Liberalisation Agreements, 26–27 October 1999.

[10] There have in fact been a number of proposals and studies relating to the environmental impact of trade liberalization. See, for example, Commission for Environmental Cooperation, *Assessing Environmental Effects of the North American Free Trade Agreement* (Montreal, Canada: 1999).

[11] Comprehensive work has been done in this area by the OECD Secretariat, which has studied the environmental effects of trade liberalization in three sectors: environmental goods and services, the freight sector, and the fossil fuel sector. See, for example, OECD, *Environmental Effects of Liberalising Trade in Fossil Fuels*, COM/TD/ENV/(98)129 (Paris: OECD, 25 November 1998).

[12] For an analysis of the environmental implications of removing trade barriers on a sector-by-sector basis, see WTO Secretariat, *Environmental Benefits of Removing Trade Restrictions and Distortions*, WT/CTE/W/67 (Geneva: WTO, 8 November 1997).

[13] Developing countries account for over half of world trade in fish and fish products; in 1996, exports exceeded imports by $17 billion. See U.N. Food and Agriculture Organization (FAO), *State of World Fisheries and Aquaculture* (Rome: FAO, 1999).

[14] One often cited estimate suggests that the order of magnitude of subsidies to the fisheries sector worldwide is in the vicinity of $54 billion per annum, representing 77 percent of the total value of fish harvested by the world's fishing fleet.

[15] See New Zealand Submission to the CTE, *The Fisheries Sector,* WT/CTE/W/52, 21 May 1997.

[16] See United States Submission to the CTE, *Environmental and Trade Benefits of Removing Subsidies in the Fisheries Sector,* WT/CTE/W/51, 19 May 1997.

[17] Reproduced in New Zealand Submission to the CTE, *Benefits of Eliminating Trade Distorting and Environmentally Damaging Subsidies in the Fisheries Sector,* WT/CTE/W/121, 28 June 1999.

[18] Ibid., page 4.

[19] See David Schorr, "Fishery Subsidies and the WTO," in Gary P. Sampson and W. Bradnee Chambers (eds.), *Trade, Environment and the Millennium* (Tokyo: United Nations University Press, 1999).

[20] See WTO Secretariat, *GATT/WTO Rules on Subsidies and Aids Granted in the Fishing Industry,* WT/CTE/W/80, 9 March, 1998.

[21] The UNEP Workshop came to a general agreement on the need to roll back subsidies in the fishing sector, for both environmental and economic reasons. It recommended that a variety of institutional options for disciplining counterproductive fishing subsidies, including action within the WTO, under existing environmental agreements, or through negotiation of a new accord.

[22] Both fisheries and agriculture have been singled out as priority areas for developing countries by the OECD, *Trade and Investment and Development: The Challenges of Policy Coherence in a Global Economy,* SG/LINKS(99) (Paris: OECD, 19 March 1999).

[23] See the WTO, *Report of the Committee on Trade and Environment to Ministers in Singapore,* WT/CTE/1, 12 November 1996.

[24] This proposition is supported by empirical work by the OECD, the U.N. Conference on Trade and Development (UNCTAD), and the FAO. See OECD, *The Environmental Effects of Trade* (Paris: OECD, 1994); UNCTAD/CONV35, "Internalization of Environmental Damages in Agriculture," 25 April 1995; FAO, 16th Regional Conference for Europe.

[25] This concern is addressed in the Decision on Measures Concerning the Possible Negative Effects of the Reform Program on Least Developed Countries and Net Food Importing Developing Countries, which was one of the decisions adopted at the Ministerial Meeting in Marrakesh.

[26] See the first of the WTO Secretariat documents in the "win-win" series, *Environmental Benefits of Removing Trade Restrictions and Distortions,* WT/CTE/W/1, 1995.

[27] See a recent Cairns Group *Communiqué,* presented to WTO High Level Symposium on Trade and Environment, Geneva (15–16 March 1999). The *Communiqué* notes that "through the use of export subsidies, other trade distorting practices, and market access barriers, these high levels of support also block valuable exports for other countries. In particular, these policies depress international prices, increase market volatility, and undermine agricultural production and rural incomes in developing countries. By blocking the contribution trade can make to

economic development, high levels of support to agriculture contribute directly to the impoverishment of developing countries." This communication points to an interesting potential coalition between agricultural exporting countries—industrial and developing—and environmental interest groups.

[28] See WTO, op. cit. note 27.

[29] Ibid.

[30] For a discussion of the background, see WTO, *APEC's "Accelerated Tariff Liberalization" (ATL) Initiative, communication from New Zealand*, WT/GC/W/138 (Geneva: WTO, 26 January 1999).

[31] Other related concerns included WTO rules that prohibit export bans of raw logs, possible future challenges to existing possibilities for government procurement preferences for forest products from sustainable forest management programs and challenges to eco-labeling schemes.

[32] See WTO, *The Energy Sector: The Case of Ethanol Fuel*, a submission by Brazil, WT/CTE/W/98 (Geneva: WTO, 30 September 1998).

[33] See OECD, *Future Liberalisation of Trade in Environmental Goods and Services: Ensuring Economic Protection as well as Economic Benefits*, COM/TD/ENV(98)37 (Paris: OECD, 4 March 1999).

[34] See WTO, *Liberalization of Trade in Environmental Goods and Services; Contribution by the United States*, WT/CTE/W/70 (Geneva: WTO, 21 November 1997); see also the WTO Secretariat, *Environmental Benefits of Removing Trade Restrictions and Distortions: Addendum on Environmental Services*, WT/CTE/W/67, add. 1, (Geneva: WTO, March 1998).

[35] Results reported in OECD, *Report on Trade and Environment: Council at Ministerial Level*, 26–27 May 199, C/MIN(99) (Paris: OECD, 12 May 1999).

[36] The importance of subsidies is also underscored in OECD, *Improving the Environment through Removing Subsidies* (Paris: OECD, 1998).

INCREASING
IMPORTANCE
OF STANDARDS

■   AS INCOMES AND PUBLIC AWARENESS INCREASE in many countries, so does concern over the protection of public health and the environment. One outcome of this is a growth in mandatory regulations, voluntary standards, and conformity assessment procedures for products or processes that could affect either health or the environment.[1] With more-sophisticated products and production processes, the complexity of regulations has also increased, along with the opportunity for these measures to be used for protectionist purposes. When standards differ between countries, they have the potential to seriously impede trade. In fact, many in the business community consider that dealing with standards in different industrial countries is the most significant barrier to trade.[2] The same is true of developing countries.[3] Thus a particularly important consideration for the maintenance of an open trading system is determining when national standards affecting trade are responding to legitimate concerns.

Concern over the implications of standards for international trade is expressed in various agreements of the World Trade Organization (WTO), especially the Sanitary and Phytosanitary (SPS) Agreement and the Technical Barriers to Trade (TBT) Agreement.[4] Both agreements seek to avoid unnecessary obstacles to trade. Yet they also recognize the sovereign right of governments to adopt whatever standards are appropriate to fulfill legitimate objectives, taking into account the risks that nonfulfillment would create.

Determining what is "appropriate" in the light of scientific evidence and what constitutes legitimacy in terms of public preferences promises to be one of the most contentious areas for environmentalists and trade officials alike. There have already been serious trade disagreements on appropriate standards for meat treated with hormones or antibiotics. Those relating to the trade in genetically modified organisms (GMOs) and trade and consumption of products derived from them involve even greater commercial, health, social, and ethical considerations. Similarly, the WTO has already struggled with the use of trade measures to promote the conservation of endangered and other species of marine life, and it may run into the same problems with measures to reduce carbon emissions in accordance with the objectives of the climate change agreements (see Chapter 6).

Although the WTO is neither a standard-setting nor a standard-enforcing body, the relevance of standards for its work can be broadly dealt with under two headings. The first relates to implementing the rules that permit national sovereignty in the choice of domestic standards without letting them be used as disguised barriers to trade. To minimize any potential problems in this respect, WTO agreements encourage members to adopt common standards established by international bodies (such as the International Organization for Standardization) or, in the absence of such a standard, to recognize the equivalence of the standards of other members. The second relates to the implications for the WTO of trade measures used to enforce international standards (such as those established by multilateral agreements), as well as unilateral trade measures used to enforce the international adoption of preferred standards where such agreements do not exist. In this chapter I address the first category of standards, and in Chapter 6 I deal with the second, although there is certainly an overlap.

The relative weight assigned to science and societal choice in the determination of standards underpins much of the possible future disagreement over their legitimacy within the context of dispute resolution in the WTO.[5] There is a recognition that this issue will certainly emerge as developments in biotechnology proceed. For example, the G8 Cologne Communiqué of June 1999 notes that: "Because trade is increasingly global, the consequences of developments in biotechnology must be dealt with at the national and international levels in all the appropriate fora. We are committed to a science-based, rules-based approach to addressing these issues."[6]

Numerous questions surround these issues: What minimum degree of scientific validation is required for a trading partner to be obliged to accept a standard as being appropriate? What is the role of "precaution" if there is insufficient scientific evidence to establish a standard but substantial potential consequences to society of not setting such a standard? Who has the burden of proof in demonstrating that there is—or is not—a real risk? It would be most surprising if matters relating to risk assessment and risk management do not become increasingly important in WTO legal proceedings and, as a consequence, the agreements that deal with them.

This chapter begins, therefore, with a brief discussion of precaution and the relevant aspects of risk before turning to the agreements that relate to standards and how they bear on the environment. Some of the very practical implications of those agreements—such as labeling requirements—are also addressed.

· ·

MANAGING RISK

■ RISK ASSESSMENT IS THE SCIENTIFIC DETERMINATION of the relationship between cause and effect in situations where adverse effects can occur. It is hard to imagine a role for the WTO in this. Risk management, on the other hand, is the process of identifying, evaluating, selecting, and implementing measures to reduce risk.[7] Managing risk entails ascertaining what constitutes an acceptable level of risk and then setting the necessary standards to permit the risk to be managed appropriately.

The setting of standards requires not only scientific evidence but also the establishment of a level of protection that is considered appropriate by society. In some instances, a particular standard may not be appropriate across countries as the physical conditions may differ between areas in the light of scientific risk assessment. Absorptive capacities for air pollution, for example, differ between countries depending on their physical characteristics. Although such differences across countries can presumably be measured objectively, this is not necessarily the case with respect to how different societies wish to manage the risk. It has been observed that scientific evidence would certainly support the notion that cigarette smoking poses a greater risk to health than eating hormone-treated meat. Yet in the European Union (EU), the first is tolerated and the second is banned.[8] The importance that the public assigns to certain risks and how to manage them cannot be objectively evaluated by science; thus enacting legislation to limit risk in the absence of scientific evidence is a political decision.

The precautionary principle is an increasingly important concept in risk assessment. According to the Rio Declaration on Environment and Development signed at the U.N. Conference on Environment and

Development in 1992: "In order to protect the environment, the precautionary approach shall be widely applied by States according to their capabilities. Where there are threats of serious or irreversible damage, lack of full scientific certainty shall not be used as a reason for postponing cost-effective measures to prevent environmental degradation."[9] This responds to the gap between banning a product or procedure until science has proved it is harmless and not banning it until science has proved that there is a real risk. The theoretical underpinnings of this principle are, however, elusive and difficult to define. One study on its interpretation notes that precaution is a "culturally framed concept . . . muddled in policy advice and subject to the whims of international diplomacy and the unpredictable public mood over the true cost of sustainable living."[10] Thus the precautionary principle has flexibility in its application and can fit many existing policies.

The principle has already secured its place in a number of international agreements. The Biodiversity Convention, for instance, states that "where there is a threat of significant reduction or loss of biological diversity, lack of full scientific certainty should not be used as a reason for postponing measures to avoid or minimise such a threat."[11] The principle is also enunciated in the Amsterdam Treaty, which amended the Treaty of Rome to read as follows: "Community policy on the environment shall aim at a high level of protection taking into account the diversity of situations in the various regions of the Community. It shall be based on the precautionary principle and on the principles that preventative action should be taken, that environmental damage should as a priority be rectified at source and that the polluter should pay."[12]

Not surprisingly, there is no consensus with respect to accepting the precautionary principle as a basis for establishing obligations in national and international rules. The potential implications for a number of WTO agreements are significant. The WTO should avoid finding itself in a situation where it is the arbiter in such controversies. This appears inevitable, however, given the current state of affairs. Indeed, the WTO has already been described as the "World Trans Science Organization, a global metaregulator." It resolves "scientific issues such as carcinogenicity, adopts policies concerning the acceptable levels of risk or scientific uncertainty, and makes decisions about appropriate levels of health and safety."[13] With negotiations under way on how to deal with trade in GMOs and products derived from them, this may only be the first shot in the battle that lies ahead.

SANITARY AND
PHYTOSANITARY MEASURES

■ THE AGREEMENT ON SANITARY AND PHYTOSANITARY Measures was an outcome of the Uruguay Round of trade negotiations.[14] It applies to measures to protect humans, animals, and plants from additives, contaminants, toxins, or disease-causing organisms in food substances as well as from the spread of disease by pests, animals, or plants. Although the agreement explicitly recognizes members' sovereign rights to take measures that may restrict trade, any such steps must be based on scientific evidence and taken in accordance with the traditional national treatment and most-favored-nation (MFN) principles of other WTO agreements. Thus such measures should apply to domestically produced food or local animal and plant diseases as well as to products coming from other countries, without unjustified discrimination among foreign sources of supply. In short, the SPS Agreement requires that potentially trade-restrictive measures be applied to local and foreign products for no other purpose than that of ensuring food safety and animal and plant health, that any such measures do not result in unjustified barriers to trade, and that they be based on scientific evidence.

Perhaps the most important objective of the agreement is to reduce the arbitrariness of governments' decisions by clarifying which factors to take into account when adopting health protection measures. In particular, measures taken to ensure food safety and animal and plant health should be based on the analysis and assessment of objective and accurate scientific data. Thus an important question in managing risks to human, animal, and plant life and health is deciding on risk levels and the appropriate standards to adopt to manage that risk.

International standard-setting organizations offer ready-made yardsticks. The SPS Agreement explicitly refers to three such groups whose activities are considered relevant in meeting its objectives: the Codex Alimentarius Commission, a joint effort of the Food and Agriculture Organization (FAO) and the World Health Organization; the International Office of Epizootics (OIE); and the international and regional organizations operating within the framework of the FAO International Plant Protection Convention (IPPC). Many WTO members are involved in those fora, and their scientists and health experts participated in the development of these voluntary international standards.

From a rules perspective, the fact that the SPS Agreement and the WTO were created at the same time is particularly important for at least two reasons. First, domestic standards to protect human, animal, and plant life could not be challenged under the General Agreement on Tariffs and Trade (GATT) if the standards were applied in a nondiscriminatory manner. As long as both domestic and imported goods were treated as "like products" and the treatment was equal, the scientific justification for such measures was not called into question.

One well-known, high-profile case that exemplifies the impact of this provision is the long-standing U.S. challenge to European regulations on hormone-treated meat. European measures could not be challenged by the United States under the GATT because the only applicable GATT clause at that stage was the national treatment obligation, which required that imported products be treated no differently than domestic ones. As meat products containing hormones were also banned domestically, there was no violation of the GATT nondiscrimination principle.[15]

With the entry into force of the WTO and the SPS Agreement in January 1995, however, the legal framework changed, allowing governments to challenge regulations based on food safety even when there was no discrimination between imported and domestic food substances. It has, in fact, been argued that one of the main U.S. motivations for negotiating the SPS Agreement in the Uruguay Round was to have the means to tackle the EU on hormone regulations.[16] With the entry into force of the SPS Agreement, scientific evidence was now required to justify domestic regulation.

Second, prior to the WTO's entry into force, international standards designed to protect animal, plant, and human life and health were adopted by governments on a voluntary basis. These norms have now in effect been conferred a new status by the SPS Agreement, although not explicitly made compulsory. When adopting such norms, a WTO member is presumed to be in full compliance with the SPS Agreement.

As conditions differ between countries, protection levels can be established that exceed international standards that are judged not to provide an acceptable level of protection. But if challenged, these measures must be supported by scientific evidence based on an objective assessment of the potential health risks involved. When introducing a standard that is more trade-restrictive than Codex, OIE, or IPPC, the SPS Agreement calls for measures based on the analysis and assessment of objective and accurate scientific data.[17] In the absence of an international standard, each country must conduct its own risk assessment and determine its "acceptable level of risk." These commonly include substantial safety margins as a precautionary measure. Once a government has determined its appropriate level of sanitary and phytosanitary protection, however, to be consistent with the WTO it should not choose a measure that is more stringent and trade-restrictive than necessary. Thus the evaluation of this is important in determining the measure, the effects of which should be proportional to the risk.

The SPS Agreement allows countries to take measures in cases of emergency where sufficient scientific evidence does not yet exist to support definitive measures. This is how the agreement deals with precaution in an operational sense. Following the scare in 1996 relating to bovine spongiform encephalopathy ("mad cow disease"), and in the absence of sufficient scientific evidence, several emergency bans were introduced. In accordance with the SPS Agreement, however, these could only be provisional. In the long term, governments must conduct scientific risk assessment and adapt their measures accordingly, although there is no determination as to how long "provisional" may be.

Thus the role of science is important in the SPS Agreement not only for the setting of standards and deviation from them but also for precautionary emergency measures. Herein lies the problem. In the interface between science and regulation, there is the critical question of the manner in which the risk is to be managed. This complicates matters enormously, and, as noted earlier, different societies have different preferences for the management of risk. It also creates the possibility of abuse of measures for protectionist purposes.

The recent dispute on meat treated with hormones heralds future potential problems for the WTO. The EU ban on meat products containing hormones went into effect in 1989; it applied to animals treated with hormones to promote growth, as the EU maintained that there was a carcinogenic effect associated with human consumption of the hormone-treated beef. When the case was dealt with by a WTO panel, the panelists rejected the EU arguments due to a lack of scientific evidence of a health and safety risk. They concluded this after consulting scientific experts, and there was general agreement that the hormones posed no risk. The panel did not consider information presented by public interest groups. In the proceedings, international standards played an important role—in particular, the use of the Codex benchmark standard. The EU argued that Codex did not represent a consensus-based standard for minimum residue levels of growth-promoting hormones, because it was adopted by a vote of 33–29, with 7 abstentions. From an operational perspective, the SPS Agreement thus required that the EU implement food safety standards when the minimum levels were agreed to by fewer than half of the Codex experts. The EU argued that being obligated to accept standards that were not approved on a consensus basis was far from the consensus-based notion of WTO rules.

The panel also considered whether the precautionary principle could provide justification for the ban in the absence of scientifically based risk assessment. It noted that the precautionary principle was incorporated into the SPS Agreement through the use of emergency measures permitting members to provisionally introduce measures that are not supported by "sufficient" scientific evidence until this evidence is obtained. In the hormone case, emergency measures as such were not under discussion, because the ban did not relate to "provisional regulations." The EU Directive was a definitive regulation.

The panel report was referred to the appellate body, which agreed that the specific wording in the SPS Agreement prevailed over the precautionary principle. However, neither the panel nor the appellate body addressed whether scientific risk assessment and the precautionary principle were potentially at odds. The EU was restricting the importation of hormone-treated beef when scientific risk assessments could not support the fear of society toward the potential risk involved. In fact, the appellate body concluded that the precautionary principle awaits confirmation as a customary principle of international law.

. . . .

TECHNICAL BARRIERS . TO TRADE

■   THE WTO TECHNICAL BARRIERS TO TRADE Agreement establishes obligations to ensure that voluntary standards, mandatory regulations, and conformity assessment procedures are not prepared, adopted, or applied with the view or effect of creating unnecessary obstacles to international trade. In line with the concept of proportionality, avoiding unnecessary obstacles to trade means that when preparing a technical regulation to achieve a certain policy objective, the government should choose the approach that has the least restrictive impact on trade. The conventional GATT disciplines of MFN and national treatment apply to technical regulations. For example, the agreement states that in respect to their technical regulations, products imported from the territory of any member be accorded treatment no less favorable than that accorded to like products of national origin and to like products originating in any other country. Similar provisions apply to standards.

The agreement draws a distinction between a standard and a technical regulation on the basis of compliance and enforcement.[18] Although conformity with standards is voluntary, technical regulations are by their nature mandatory.[19] Technical regulations and conformity assessment procedures are covered through the main body of the agreement, but standards are covered through a Code of Good Practice for the Preparation, Adoption, and Application of Standards, which is an annex. Most of the principles applied by the agreement to technical regulations also apply to standards through this Code. All governmental as well as nongovernmental standard-setting bodies at the national and regional level are invited to accept to Code and to abide by its provisions.[20]

The distinction in compliance requirements has particularly important implications for international trade. If an imported product does not meet the requirements of a technical regulation, it will not be allowed for sale. But in the case of standards, noncomplying imported products are allowed into the market, although they may well be shunned by consumers.[21] For this reason, voluntary standards can operationally have the same effect as mandatory regulations.

The agreement encourages WTO members to use, whenever appropriate, relevant standards or conformity assessment guides or recommendations issued by international standardizing bodies as a basis for their own regulations and procedures. The use of internationally recognized standards is presumed not to constitute an unnecessary barrier to trade. Nevertheless, the agreement acknowledges that there are good reasons for mandatory regulations and voluntary standards to differ between countries. It states that: "no country should be prevented from taking measures necessary to ensure the quality of its exports, or for the protection of human, animal, and plant life or health, of the environment, or for the prevention of deceptive practices, at the levels it considers appropriate." The agreement also states that standards may differ between countries due to differences in taste or levels of income, as well as geographic and other factors. Thus, legitimate differences can be fully reflected in domestic regulations. Although this offers a high degree of flexibility in the preparation, adoption, and application of national technical regulations, it also raises the questions of which differences are "legitimate," what criterion establishes legitimacy, and which standards create unnecessary obstacles to trade.[22]

Do national regulations frequently differ from international standards for environmental reasons? One way to answer this question is to examine the notifications that have been made to the WTO Secretariat under the obligation of the TBT Agreement. If national technical regulations differ from international standards and have an important effect on international trade, then other WTO members should be notified about them through the Secretariat. As part of the notification process, the objective of the measure must be identified.

According to a study by the WTO Secretariat, a growing number of such notifications relate to the environment.[23] In 1998, there were 2,140 notifications in total under the various obligations of the WTO agreements.[24] In the same year, there were 648 notifications under the TBT Agreement, 15 percent of which identified protection of the environment as the main or one of the main purposes for notification. It could be argued that what is more significant than the share of total notifications is the fact that the number more than doubled in the past four years. The principal reasons given for diverging from international standards included waste management; energy efficiency; providing for environmental management systems; eco-taxes; and soil, water, and air pollution.[25]

Does it matter that so many environmental standards differ? The answer is both yes and no. Ostensibly there is no problem, as there has never been a dispute panel addressing whether obligations of the TBT Agreement have been breached. Nevertheless, one-third of the requests for consultations under the Dispute Settlement Understanding cite a violation of the TBT Agreement. At the stage of the panel process, however, references to the TBT Agreement have been dropped, as other general WTO obligations can be cited instead, such as the failure to respect national treatment and MFN treatment.[26] Testing the TBT Agreement is perhaps avoided because the outcome is unpredictable, given the lack of precedent.

PRODUCTS, PROCESSES,
AND LABELS

■ THE OBJECTIVE OF THE TBT AGREEMENT is to ensure the legitimacy of regulations and standards, including those for the protection of human, animal, and plant life or health and the environment. There is little doubt that the agreement will become increasingly important in future disputes between WTO members as disagreement over the legitimacy of certain technical regulations and standards widens. To cite but one example, the current and potential importance of trade in biotechnology products is enormous, including GMOs and products derived from them. The public reaction as to the acceptability of GMOs and their products differs greatly across countries and is reflected in very different legislation relating to biotechnology. This is already apparent; the liberal views of countries such as the United States and Canada differ significantly from those (mostly in the EU) who are hostile to the cultivation and import of GMOs and products derived from them.

Although the importance of the TBT Agreement will increase in the future, the discussion in both the Committee on Trade and Environment (CTE) and the TBT Committee has revealed a marked divergence of views with respect to some of the key provisions. Much of this relates to disagreement over the coverage of the disciplines of the agreement.[27] What is not contested is that the TBT covers regulations and standards as they relate to products. But there is no such consensus as to its coverage of standards and regulations relating to the processes and methods that produced the product, unless the method of production is "incorporated" into the product (that is, the production method is evident in the product itself).[28]

The manner in which this debate is resolved will have major practical implications in a number of areas of considerable commercial significance. For example, the legality under WTO of many labeling schemes is at stake. Voluntary and mandatory labeling schemes are covered by the TBT Agreement and the Code of Good Practice.[29] They are seen by many as a market-based response to dealing with differing views on potential health and environment matters by offering information to consumers and providing the basis for well-informed choices. Eco-labeling schemes, for instance, provide consumers with information about how goods have been produced to help them identify products that have harmed (or helped) the environment during production either in their own countries or abroad. According to the CTE, well-designed eco-labeling schemes can be effective instruments of environmental policy to encourage the development of an environmentally conscious consumer public.[30]

As the disciplines of the TBT Agreement apply to labeling schemes, this has important implications. According to the agreement, they should be applied in a nondiscriminatory manner, not create unnecessary obstacles to trade, and not be more trade-restrictive than necessary to fulfill a legitimate objective. If based on international standards, they are presumed not to create an unnecessary obstacle to trade; members are required to adhere to notification, publication, and delays in entry-into-force procedures associated with the adoption of new measures. For voluntary labeling schemes, if they are administered by the central government, the government is required to accept and comply with the "Code of Good Practice," which contains the same broad obligations as those required of mandatory schemes.[31] Although there is agreement that labeling schemes relating to the characteristics of the product are covered by agreement and its code, this is not the case for labels that describe the manner in which a product was produced. This clearly is important for the treatment of eco-labeling schemes in the WTO if, for example, they are based on a life-cycle approach.

Although this is an important consideration in itself, there is another consideration of equal importance. Even if labels describing the manner in which products are produced are covered by the disciplines of the agreement, are they consistent with it? In other words, are process-based eco-labeling schemes legal in the WTO?

Those arguing that they are illegal point out that both the GATT and the TBT Agreement prohibit discrimination between "like" products.[32] Members are to ensure that in respect to technical regulations and voluntary standards, products imported from any member are to be accorded treatment no less favorable than that accorded to like products of national origin and to like products originating in any other country. The question of interpretation is whether the likeness of "products" extends to the likeness of the extent to which products may be differentiated based on production criteria that do not affect their characteristics. It has been argued in the CTE, particularly by developing countries, that labels based on production and process methods are inconsistent with the GATT/WTO interpretation of like products, and therefore actionable.

In this view, if process-based standards were both covered by the TBT Agreement and consistent with it, this would bring advantages (such as greater transparency, notification of the schemes) but would also create a precedent for new WTO disciplines that relate to the manner in which traded goods are produced. This is something that most if not all developing countries wish to avoid. In the case of environmental standards, for example, it would mean the determination of "appropriate" production methods for their exports by those outside their borders. It is argued that this could result in the imposition of standards that are inappropriate for local conditions, lead to protectionists abuse, and constitute an encroachment on national sovereignty. (See also Chapter 7.)

It is important to note that like other WTO rules, those contained in the TBT Agreement address the actions of member governments. As a result, purely private labeling programs with no government involvement are unlikely to be considered as subject to the disciplines of the agreement. There is, however, a gray area. Nongovernmental organizations urge governments to take reasonable measures to ensure compliance with the provisions, and some government procurement schemes require voluntary labeling on the part of suppliers. In addition, if a WTO member government were to participate in some manner in the labeling program, it is possible to foresee a scenario in which a voluntary label may no longer be considered private by other GATT/WTO members.

Although no labeling case involving an alleged violation of the TBT Agreement has been brought to the WTO panel process yet, storm clouds are on the horizon.[33] In recent meetings of the TBT Committee, the United States and Canada expressed concern over the EU regulation on the labeling of food products containing or derived from genetically modified soya or maize. The EU requires foodstuffs and food ingredients containing traces of modified DNA or protein to be labeled as "produced with genetically modified soya/maize." The United States and Canada argued that such labels were unnecessary technical barriers to trade since no scientific reason existed to differentiate between foodstuffs produced with genetically modified crops and "normal" maize/soya. The United States also questioned the feasibility of developing reliable and commercially practical tests for detecting DNA or protein resulting from genetic modification, especially at very low thresholds.

NOTES

[1] Unless otherwise specified, the term "standard" will be used to cover both mandatory regulations and voluntary standards.

[2] As part of the Cecchini Report, 11,000 business leaders in the European Community (EC) were asked to rank the importance of national standards and regulations, along with seven other general categories of trade impediments, as a hindrance to intra-Community trade. In four major countries, business leaders ranked divergent national standards and regulations at the top of their list of internal market barriers. The EC-wide average of all responses placed standards as the second most important obstacle. For a description of the results of the Cecchini Report, see OECD, *OECD Consumer Product Safety Standards and Conformity Assessment: Issues in a Global Market Place* (Paris: OECD, 1996), pp. 35–37.

[3] See a study by the World Trade Organization (WTO) Secretariat on the situation in developing countries: WTO, *Technical Barriers to the Market Access of Developing Countries*, WT/CTE/101 (Geneva: WTO, 25 January 1999).

[4] The Trade-Related Intellectual Property Rights Agreement also establishes minimum standards for the protection of intellectual property. These are not addressed here.

[5] For an in-depth discussion of the implications of differing standards and societal choice across countries for the General Agreement on Tariffs and Trade (GATT) and other WTO Agreements, see Jagdish Bhagwati and T.N. Srinivasan, "Trade and Environment: Does Environmental Diversity Detract from the Case for Free Trade?" in Jagdish Bhagwati and Robert Hudec (eds.), *Fair Trade and Harmonisation: Prerequisites for Free Trade?* (Cambridge, MA: The MIT Press, 1996).

[6] For the text and discussion of the G8 Cologne Communiqué, see Institute for Trade and Sustainable Development, "G7–G8 Endorse Trade-Environment Link," in *Bridges Between Trade and Sustainable Development*, Year 3, No. 5 (June 1999).

[7] National Research Council, *Risk Assessment in the Federal Government* (Washington, DC: NRC, 1983).

[8] See Steve Charnovitz, "The World Trade Organization, Meat Hormones and Food Safety," *International Trade Reporter*, Vo. 14, No. 41 (15 October 1998).

[9] See the Report of United Nations Conference on Environment and Development, Annex 1, *Rio Declaration on Environment and Development*, Rio de Janeiro, 3–14 June 1992, Principle 15.

[10] T. O'Riordan and J. Cameron, "The History and Contemporary Significance of the Precautionary Principle," in T. O'Riordan and J. Cameron (eds.), *Interpreting the Precautionary Principle* (London: Earthscan, 1994).

[11] See U.N. Environment Programme, *Convention on Biological Diversity*, Convention, Preamble, Paragraph 9, UNEP/CBD/94/1 (Geneva: UNEP, November 1994).

[12] For an elaboration, see European Commission, Directorate General XXIV, *Guidelines on the Application of the Precautionary Principle*, HB/hb D(98) (Brussels: European Commission, 17 October 1998).

[13] See Vern R. Walker, "Keeping the WTO from Becoming the World Trans Science Organization: Scientific Uncertainty, Science Policy, and Factfinding in the Growth Hormones Dispute,"

Cornell International Law Journal, Vol. 31 (1998), pp. 251–320. Questions of trans-science in this context are considered to be "those which can be asked of science and yet which cannot be answered by science."

[14] For a description of the SPS Agreement and its interpretation in WTO cases, see Steve Charnovitz, "Improving the Agreement on Sanitary and Phytosanitary Standards," in Gary P. Sampson and W. Bradnee Chambers (eds.), *Trade, Environment and the Millennium* (Tokyo: United Nations University Press, 1999).

[15] Charnovitz, op. cit. note 8.

[16] See Marsha A. Echols, "Sanitary and Phytosanitary Measures," in Terence P. Stewart (ed.), *The World Trade Organization: Multilateral Trade Framework for the 21st Century and U.S Implementing Legislation* (Washington, DC: Section on International Law and Practice, American Bar Association, 1996).

[17] See WTO Secretariat, *Sanitary and Phytosanitary Measures*, WTO Agreement Series No. 4, WTO, Geneva, 1998.

[18] Most technical regulations and standards adopted by countries are aimed at protecting human safety or health. Examples abound: requirements that motor vehicles carry reflective devices to prevent road accidents; labeling requirements for cigarettes, drugs, and alcoholic beverages; electric insulation requirements; car emission standards; limits on the use of certain dying and tanning materials.

[19] For the purposes of the TBT Agreement, a technical regulation is a document that lays down characteristics for products or related processes and production methods, including the applicable administrative provisions, with which compliance is mandatory. A standard is defined to be a document approved by a recognized body, that provides, for common and repeated use, rules, guidelines, or characteristics for products or related processes and production methods with which compliance is not mandatory.

[20] As most of the bodies that develop standards tend to be nongovernmental, the code was created to bring their work under the purview of the agreement.

[21] For example, some consumers may shun an energy-intensive air-conditioning system that has not met a voluntary standard for energy consumption.

[22] As part of the realization that standards will differ among WTO members, the agreement encourages members, in cases where they do not adopt the same standards, to recognize foreign regulations as equivalent to their own. Members are also to consult with other members for the conclusion of agreements on the mutual recognition of standards and conformity assessment results.

[23] See WTO Secretariat, *Provisions of the Multilateral Trading System With Respect to the Transparency of Trade Measures Used for Environmental Purposes and Environmental Measures and Requirements Which Have Significant Trade Effects*, WT/CTE/W/77 (Geneva: WTO, 28 June 1999).

[24] These notifications serve different purposes, depending on the agreements.

[25] By way of comparison, 36 of the 90 notifications under the Subsidies and Countervailing Measures Agreement were environment-related, covering programs such as waste management, incentives for pollution control, and subsidies for pollution prevention. In the case of the Agreement on Agriculture, 22 of the 190 notifications related to environment measures,

including domestic support for research, payments for soil conservation, promotion of sustainable use of natural resources, and payments for environmentally friendly wine growing methods.

[26] A first exception to the rule is the current complaint by Canada lodged against France relating to asbestos standards.

[27] For a comprehensive discussion of the positions of WTO members on the interpretation of the TBT Agreement with respect to eco-labeling see Doaa Abdel Motaal, "The Agreement on Technical Barriers to Trade, the Committee on Trade and the Environment, and Eco-labelling," in Sampson and Chambers, op. cit. note 14.

[28] Standards and regulations relating to processes and production methods are covered by the agreement if they are apparent in the product itself. For example, a regulation relating to motor fuel could be established on the basis of its chemical composition or the manner in which the fuel was produced. The regulation relating to the production process would be covered by the agreement only if the process affected the chemical composition of the fuel. See the WTO Secretariat study relating to standards, "Negotiating History of the Coverage of the Agreement on Technical Barriers to Trade with Regard to Labelling Requirements, Voluntary Standards and Processes and Production Methods Unrelated to Product Characteristics," WT/CTE/W/10 (Geneva: WTO, 29 August 1995).

[29] According to the WTO Secretariat, op. cit. note 28, mandatory labeling requirements are subject to the provisions of the TBT Agreement regardless of the kind of information provided on the label. By implication, voluntary labeling standards are subject to the provisions the Code of Good Practice for the Preparation, Adoption and Application of Standards regardless of the kind of information provided on the label.

[30] See the CTE, *Report (1996) of the Committee on Trade and Environment*, WT/CTE/1 (Geneva: CTE, November 1996).

[31] The government is also to urge private or nongovernmental programs to comply with the Code of Good Practice.

[32] As noted elsewhere, under GATT's most-favored-nation clause, WTO members must accord treatment that is no less favorable to like imported products. Under the national treatment clause, they must accord treatment that is no less favorable to imported products than that which they give to like domestically produced products.

[33] A recent submission by the United States to the TBT Committee points to the potential growing importance of this problem. It is manifested in the increasing number of notifications related to GMOs.

Chapter 6
Multilateral
Environmental
Agreements

DIFFERING RULES
AND OBJECTIVES

■   THE G8 COLOGNE COMMUNIQUÉ OF JUNE 1999 reflects a long-standing concern about a potential lack of coherence between multilateral environmental agreements (MEAs) and World Trade Organization (WTO) rules. It states that: "We agree that environmental considerations should be taken fully into account in the upcoming round of WTO negotiations. This should include a clarification of the relationship between both multilateral and environmental agreements and key environmental principles, and WTO rules."[1] This same concern was expressed in the Marrakesh Ministerial Decision of April 1994, which served as a basis for the agenda for the Committee of Trade and Environment (CTE).

Since the CTE was established, one of the most actively discussed items has been the relationship between WTO provisions and the use of trade measures in MEAs.[2] Indeed, it is difficult to imagine any potential aspect of the relationship that has not been intensively discussed or any solution to the problem that has yet to be proposed by WTO members.[3] Notwithstanding this exhaustive treatment of the topic, no action has been taken by the CTE.

At the time of the creation of the CTE, the concern stemmed from the fact that a number of MEAs contained provisions relating to trade that were inconsistent with the rules of the WTO. For example, the Montreal Protocol on Substances That Deplete the Ozone Layer, the Convention on International Trade in Endangered Species of Wild Fauna and Flora, and the Basel Convention on the Control of the Transboundary Movements of Hazardous Wastes and Their Disposal all use a combination of trade measures and incentives that are potentially at variance with the WTO in order to reach their intended environmental objectives.[4] The nature of the measures differ, as well as the conditions under which the measures are taken.[5]

Because the WTO and MEAs represent two different bodies of international law, the relationship between them should be fully understood and coherent. In seeking coherence, there are many practical implications: What happens when measures taken in accordance with an MEA violate a government's obligations under the WTO and vice versa? Under which body of law would disputes be resolved?

Different views have been advanced in the CTE about how possible inconsistencies between WTO rules and those in an MEA could be addressed.[6] In a broad perspective, it could be argued that no real problem exists, since few MEAs contain trade provisions and no trade dispute has arisen over the use of those provisions. This argument probably goes far in explaining why, in spite of the importance of a potential conflict, no action has been taken by the CTE. An alternative view recognizes the increasing commercial and political importance of some MEAs dealing with transborder problems currently under negotiation, such as those to address biosafety and climate change. This school of thought considers it important to ensure that the appropriate measures are in place to avoid any conflict of the trade and environmental regimes, and to provide greater certainty as concern grows about the collective impact of individual countries on the global commons.

The numerous proposals that have emerged on how to accommodate the relationship between MEAs and the WTO differ greatly in scope and level of ambition, but they are bound by one common characteristic—that consensus-based agreements are the best way to deal with global environmental problems. In fact, while not stated as such, a clear policy view that emerged from the CTE has been that the WTO has no expertise in the matters addressed in MEAs and that it supports the use of MEAs to deal with global problems. In the area of agreements to deal with the environment, the WTO has in fact proved to be the antithesis of the body trying to extend its reach into other areas that it is accused of being. This approach has been consolidated in recent appellate body rulings, such as the shrimp-turtle dispute, where the appellate body reprimanded the United States for not having sought to create an international environment agreement in fishing practices to deal with the problem at hand.[7]

Although no dispute has ever been brought to the WTO that concerns an inconsistency between a MEA and WTO rules, there are no grounds for complacency. The commercial, political, and social importance of some of the MEAs currently under discussion have brought a new urgency to addressing the potential problems that may arise through a lack of coherence between the different bodies of law. As will be discussed, even if they are not specifically provided for in climate change agreements, measures will be taken to mitigate climate change that may well be at variance with WTO rules.

It has also been argued that the WTO rules and the objectives of some MEAs are not mutually supportive. The view has been expressed in the CTE, for example, that the Trade-Related Intellectual Property Rights Agreement of the WTO is at variance with the objectives of the Convention on Biological Diversity, with protection of the rights of indigenous people, with transfer of environmentally sound technology, and, to the extent that patents apply to life forms, with protection of biodiversity. Similarly, as restrictions are sought by some on trade in genetically modified organisms and products derived from them under the January 2000 Biosafety Protocol, serious consideration should be given to the future relationship of the protocol with the WTO. The appreciation of these potential problems may well be one reason the issue was given priority in the G8 Communiqué.

In this chapter I identify and elaborate on the principal issues that arise when examining the possible lack of coherence between MEA and WTO rules. I also examine the options available for creating a "framework" to accommodate these two bodies of law. To give the discussion a real world context, particular attention is paid to the ongoing climate change negotiations, which serve as a good example of potential inconsistencies. Since the climate change agreement is still evolving through work on important components such as the compliance mechanism, there is time to ensure that whatever is agreed to is coherent with the trade regime (and vice versa). In practical terms, this means making its provisions consistent with WTO provisions or getting WTO members to formally recognize any inconsistencies. Another good reason to examine this agreement is that its commercial, political, and social significance is such that a lack of coherence between the trade and climate change regimes could have serious consequences on a global scale. A clash between the rules relating to climate change and world trade should be avoided.[8] Thus, I first address the climate change rules and their possible inconsistency with the WTO before turning to the more general discussion of the options for creating a framework to deal with trade rules and environment rules.

. . . .

CLIMATE CHANGE MEASURES AND THE WTO

■   THE UNITED NATIONS FRAMEWORK CONVENTION on Climate Change (FCCC) entered into force on March 21, 1994, and so far some 175 states have ratified or acceded to it. The parties to the convention commit themselves to cooperating to promote a supportive and open economic system. They clearly recognize that measures taken to address climate change problems have the potential to be used for trade protectionism. So the treaty specifically states that measures taken to combat climate change, including unilateral ones, should not constitute a means of arbitrary or unjustifiable discrimination or a disguised restriction on international trade.[9] Unlike the MEAs mentioned earlier, the convention does not provide for any specific trade-related environmental measures.

The convention is—as its name indicates—a framework only, and specific provisions on the nature of commitments by members and legal instruments such as compliance procedures are being elaborated in subsequent protocols. The Conference of the Parties (COP)—the decision-making body of the convention—held its third session in December 1997, during which 160 industrial and developing countries adopted the Kyoto Protocol by consensus. Its centerpiece is the commitment for industrial countries to reduce their collective emissions of greenhouse gases by at least 5 percent below 1990 levels by 2008–12.[10] The protocol will enter into force following the ratification from 55 countries that accounted for at least 55 percent of carbon emissions in 1990. In November 1998, at its fourth session, the COP agreed on the Buenos Aires Plan of Action for finalizing the protocol's outstanding details by the end of 2000.

The Kyoto Protocol provides for mechanisms through which parties can implement their emissions commitments. First, domestic policies and measures are provided for. In an operational sense, these may well be the most important means used by the parties to reduce emissions. The measures covered by this provision are not specified in the protocol, but their objectives are clear in terms of policy orientation. The signatories may take measures to promote the "progressive reduction or phasing out of market imperfections, fiscal incentives, tax and duty exemptions and subsidies in all greenhouse gas emitting sectors that run contrary to the objective of the Convention and application of market instruments."[11] This is certainly very much in line with the WTO objective of the progressive removal of trade restrictions and distortions, and more particularly with the discussion in the CTE of government distortions that can adversely affect both trade and the environment (see Chapter 4). The protocol provides further formal assurance that the intention is to avoid use of trade-distorting measures; parties shall strive to implement policies and measures "in such a way to minimize adverse effects . . . on international trade."[12] As with the FCCC itself, the Kyoto Protocol does not provide for any trade measures.

To achieve the emission reductions and policy direction described, a wide variety of measures (see Box 6–1) will be taken that may well affect the costs of production of traded goods and therefore the competitive position of producers in the world market. Examples include energy, carbon, and other taxes; mandatory and voluntary standards; subsidies for environmentally friendly production processes; labeling and certification schemes; and the sale and transfer of emission permits within or between groups of countries. Offsetting measures will be called for by those whose competitive position is adversely affected by cheaper imports not subject to the same measures in the country of origin. There is certainly the potential for such taxes and other measures to be inconsistent with WTO rules.[13]

Although the potential for conflict may exist, it should be kept in perspective. First, the convention and the protocol both acknowledge the importance of maintaining coherence between the trade and climate change regimes. On the trade side, there have been public declarations by prominent officials to this effect.[14] Second, the negotiations on mechanisms to implement emissions reductions are ongoing, whereas the WTO agreements and the disciplines they contain are established and well known. As with any legally binding multilateral agreement, all parties to it have agreed to be subjected to the obligations of that instrument. Third, inconsistency will be a problem only if WTO-inconsistent measures are applied to WTO members that are not party to the climate change convention. As virtually all WTO members are already parties to the FCCC, it could be argued that the scope for appeal under the WTO against climate change measures authorized by the FCCC but violating WTO rules is limited. (There is no confusion for non-WTO members who are parties to the climate change agreement, as naturally they have no recourse to the WTO.)

Nevertheless, grounds for complacency do not exist. While 175 states are members of the climate change convention, considerably less than the required 55 countries have ratified the Kyoto Protocol. Although all WTO members may well eventually ratify the protocol (an event some consider increasingly unlikely), at least a potential for an incomplete overlap of membership exists. It is conceivable that WTO members that are party to the climate change agreements would apply WTO-inconsistent measures to WTO members that are not party to the FCCC and its protocols. Further, at this stage at least, the Kyoto Protocol contains no details on the precise

nature of either the domestic measures to implement emission reductions or
the flexibility mechanisms. In fact, the description of the domestic measures
that may be taken to achieve the objectives of the climate change agreement is particularly vague.[15] Parties, for example, "shall implement policies
and measures such as promotion of sustainable forms of agriculture." So far,
the status of this flexibility in the application of measures is unclear in terms
of commitments in the WTO on the Agreement on Agriculture.

It should be emphasized that there is, of course, no problem if
measures taken to achieve the climate change objectives conform to WTO
rules. Whether or not a country is a member of both agreements would appear
irrelevant. At the most basic level, lack of coherence is related to whether
the agreements have a nonoverlapping membership. In the case of a common membership, WTO-inconsistent measures (for example, discriminatory
measures) applied to other parties to the climate change agreement would not
appear to be a problem either. In such a case, by joining the climate change
agreement, WTO members would have presumably agreed to forgo their
WTO rights (that is, to be discriminated against). The real problem is WTO-
inconsistent measures applied by parties to the climate change agreement—
for example, to support sustainable agriculture—against the imports of WTO
members who have chosen not to join the climate change agreement and do
not accept the justification for the agricultural support measures.

As countries develop their national response strategies, environmental taxes that apply directly to production processes are likely to play an increasingly important role.[16] In fact, recent studies have specifically addressed the situation in which national measures, such as energy efficiency standards or carbon and energy taxes, that are not applied to imports provide foreign competitors with an economic advantage. Carbon and energy taxes have been introduced in five European countries, and all include some form of compensatory measures for domestic industries, such as total exemptions for certain sectors, reduced rates for the most energy-intensive processes, ceilings for total tax payments, or subsidies for energy audits.[17] Exemptions and other such features were introduced to accommodate competitiveness concerns of energy-intensive industries, which argued that they would suffer greatly from similar companies operating in countries without such taxation.[18]

Environmental charges and taxes are increasingly used for the pursuit of national environment policy objectives and for "internalizing" domestic environmental costs. WTO rules discipline the way in which governments impose internal taxes and charges on traded goods, either when imposed on imported products or when rebated on exports. This is of considerable importance to trade and environmental policymakers in the context of proposals to increase taxes on environmentally sensitive inputs to production, such as energy and transportation.

A good example of the application of measures in accordance with the climate change agreement that would raise fundamental problems at the level of the WTO is to be found in the WTO debate on how to deal with border tax adjustments. As far as WTO rules are concerned, governments are in principle free to operate their fiscal regime according to national preferences and constraints. They are, however, subject to rules governing the application of domestic taxes and charges to goods traded internationally. Through border tax adjustment, countries may impose domestic taxes and charges on imports, and exempt or reimburse them on exports.[19] The objective is to preserve the competitive equality between domestic and imported products.[20] Which taxes can be imposed or rebated is, however, an area of some controversy in the WTO.[21]

Although it is clear that border tax adjustment is possible for taxes levied on products, the extent to which taxes on inputs incorporated or exhausted in the production process can be adjusted at the border, whether on exports or imports, remains to be clarified.[22] This has important implications for measures to reduce greenhouse gas emissions and applied to traded goods. Taxes levied directly on products because of their physical characteristics are eligible for tax adjustment under WTO rules. In the case of imports, this could be the imposition of equivalent domestic taxes on imported "like" products—for example, on the same imported coal and petroleum. As far as exports are concerned, taxes could be rebated if they were levied on the product at the domestic level, such as rebates of domestic taxes on exported coal and petroleum. This same understanding does not, however, extend to taxes paid in the process of producing the good—for example, rebating domestic taxes applied to processes, such as indirect taxes levied because of the energy consumed or the carbon emitted in the production process.[23] Thus, a domestic tax can be applied legitimately to imported fuel, but a tax cannot be applied on the energy consumed in producing a ton of steel.[24]

In short, under existing trade rules and jurisprudence, "product" taxes and charges can be adjusted at the border, but "process" taxes and charges probably cannot. Since environmental taxes and charges are at least as much process-oriented as product-oriented, WTO rules have caused concern about the competitiveness implications for domestic producers.[25]

This distinction also has implications for WTO obligations relating to subsidies.[26] The rebate of taxes in one country that is not permitted in another can have the same effect from a commercial perspective as a subsidy. Different views have been expressed on the likely treatment under the Agreement on Subsidies of a rebate for exported products of indirect environmental taxes on a process (which is not incorporated into the characteristics of the product) in excess of the tax rebated on like products when sold for domestic consumption.[27]

Another important consideration relates to measures applied to meet the objective of the climate change agreements and the Technical Barriers to Trade Agreement. As noted in Chapter 5, the latter provides flexibility by recognizing that priorities with respect to the environment differ between countries and that this can be fully reflected in domestic regulations. Therefore it permits the adoption of different standards and regulations by WTO members. This could relate to the amount of energy used in the production of a good or the level of carbon emissions within national borders. If a country chose not to adopt a certain standard that had an important effect on emissions reduction, this may give it a certain cost advantage over competitors in the world market.

This raises a number of issues. First, as discussed in Chapter 5 of this essay, the importing country cannot apply standards requirements to the processes outside its own borders; standards can apply to domestic processes, but not those in other countries. Also, labeling imports with respect to production methods raises problems in the WTO. Next, there is clearly a subsidy issue involved as well. If a country were not to invoke exacting standards with respect to an energy-intensive production process, for example, wouldn't this constitute a subsidy to the country with the lower process standards?

There is, however, flexibility in the WTO rules to deal with situations in which countries may wish to breach WTO rules and discriminate against like products. The possibility of imposing WTO-inconsistent measures is provided for. If a product were to be treated differently at the border because of the way it was produced—emitting too much carbon, for instance—an "exception" can be sought from WTO obligations to protect human, animal, or plant life or health and the environment. (See also Chapter 7.) Exceptions are also provided for measures related to the conservation of exhaustible natural resources. This general exception provision is clearly designed to permit governments to maintain or implement laws they feel are necessary to preserve the lives of people, flora, fauna, and exhaustible natural resources.

Also, if the trade action is taken pursuant to a legal instrument addressing the reduction of greenhouse gas emissions, and if the parties consider it necessary to take such action to meet the objectives of the instrument, then added support would be given to the notion that the action is "necessary" (interpreted by WTO panels as all other options having been pursued). In the case of measures taken to protect the environment by restricting trade in goods manufactured with excessive greenhouse-gas-emitting processes, for example, this could mean that an attempt has already been made to deal with the problem through the protocol and convention addressing climate change.

But in seeking a justification for a WTO exception, what weight should be given to the existence of the convention, protocol, and any further agreements? When 55 countries accounting for at least 55 percent of carbon emissions in 1990 ratify the Kyoto Protocol, will this be enough to justify differentiated treatment for trade measures applied pursuant to the environmental agreement if, for example, they are applied to WTO members who are nonparties?

A number of important issues remain. First, if a country chose not to accept a certain standard, who would judge the appropriateness of that decision? The country may not adopt the more rigorous standard, or it may find the scientific evidence unconvincing, have a high absorptive capacity for the pollution concerned, or have other social and economic priorities. Why then should an exception be granted for another country to discriminate against it? Second, based on past experience, it would appear that the right to deviate from WTO obligations through invoking an exception is granted only with respect to the fauna and flora within the country taking the action.[28] (See also Chapter 7.)

Measures taken to affect policies elsewhere are not permitted. In the case of greenhouse gas emissions, however, production occurs in the exporting country but the problem is experienced outside its borders. The greenhouse gas emissions in the exporting country may be heating the atmosphere above the importing country; under such circumstances, how is extraterritoriality to be interpreted in a dispute resolution case?

Exceptions from WTO obligations can be sought to protect exhaustible natural resources. This, too, raises critical issues in the context of climate-change-related measures. (See Chapter 7.) Since precedents have arisen in the WTO dispute settlement process establishing that clean air is a natural resource, presumably the question could be raised as to whether a stable climate is also a natural resource that could be exhausted. Could exceptions be sought to avoid the depletion of a stable climate if it were considered a depletable natural resource?

In this respect, it is also important whether the measures for which the exception is sought are specifically mandated in the environmental agreement itself or are taken to fulfill a more general objective of the agreement, with the type of measure used being at the discretion of the countries concerned. As far as authorized measures are concerned, as noted earlier, there is virtually no guidance in the Kyoto Protocol. The protocol simply states, for example, that to promote sustainable development, each party shall implement policies and measures in accordance with national circumstances, and it provides a number of examples. These include policies or measures to enhance energy efficiency, protect and enhance carbon sinks and reservoirs, promote research and development, increase the use of new and renewable forms of energy and environmentally sound technologies, phase out fiscal incentives and exemptions in greenhouse-gas-emitting sectors, and promote the application of market instruments. Such actions are to be taken in accordance with national circumstances. Whether a specific measure taken to achieve these loose objectives is legitimized under the climate change agreement is something open to interpretation—but by whom?

Another practical consideration relating to the respective roles and importance of international agreements is how disputes get settled. This has important implications for any compliance mechanism legitimizing discrimination based on, for example, products being manufactured with excessive greenhouse-gas-emitting processes. In fact, enforcement mechanisms have already been proposed that would provide for measures that would clearly violate the WTO rules, such as trade sanctions being used to enforce emission targets in other countries.[29]

Although the specifics of the climate change compliance mechanism are still to be determined, it seems reasonable to assume that an eventual conflict between WTO members who have ratified the protocol should be pursued under the climate change dispute settlement procedures. If, however, the agreement does not provide for the trade measures under dispute, then what is permissible under the WTO is relevant. In a dispute between two WTO members (one of which has not ratified a legal instrument to address climate change) over trade measures applied pursuant to the instrument, the WTO would provide the only available dispute settlement mechanism, since one party would have no rights under or access to the climate change dispute settlement mechanism. It has been noted in the CTE that in such circumstances, it would be important for the WTO Dispute Settlement Body to avoid becoming involved in pure environmental conflicts, but a WTO dispute settlement panel could seek relevant environmental expertise and technical advice.

This discussion has flagged only a selection of the issues that may have to be taken into account for the successful cohabitation of the trade and climate change regimes. It is certainly not meant to be comprehensive, and it relates only to domestic measures, not the "flexibility" mechanisms. There could be potential problems here also. To conclude this section, an example of how WTO disciplines could be relevant for one of the flexibility mechanisms is discussed—namely, emissions trading.

Under an international emissions trading regime, industrial countries could buy and sell emissions credits among themselves. They will also be able to acquire "emission reduction units" by financing certain kinds of projects in other countries. As far as tradable emission permits are concerned, this is a new area of international policy. One question that has sparked a great deal of interest is whether tradable emission schemes fall under the WTO General Agreement on Trade in Services (GATS). With a question as basic as this, it is perhaps best to go back to first principles and ask what GATS actually covers.

Contrary to what the name implies, the General Agreement on Trade in Services does not apply to services. It applies, in fact, to measures affecting trade in services. This distinction is important for those wishing to establish the relevance of the GATS for emissions trading. A "measure," in this case, is any government regulation that affects trade in services.[30] And "trade" is defined as the cross-border sale of a service (telecommunications), a consumer moving to a foreign country to consume a service (tourism), the commercial establishment of a foreign service supplier (establishing a foreign branch bank), or a service supplier traveling abroad to sell a service (a consultant working overseas).

The sectoral coverage of services activities has been determined through negotiators' agreement to a list of activities to which the GATS obligations apply. Thus the real question to address with respect to the application of GATS to matters relevant to climate change agreements is less one of coverage than of the activities related to emissions trading services to which GATS would apply. There are many. In fact, all services that relate to emissions trading provide examples: services relating to trading in financial derivations (such as brokerage services), consultancy services, accounting services, and a vast array of other "traded" services.

. . . .

RECONCILING MEAs
AND TRADE RULES

■ WHAT HAS CLEARLY EMERGED FROM DISCUSSIONS in the CTE is that members accept that MEAs are the best way to coordinate policy action to tackle global and transboundary environmental problems cooperatively. Also, WTO members have made it clear that they do not want the WTO to become an environmental policymaking organization or standards enforcement agency. WTO members are free to adopt nondiscriminatory trade measures to protect their domestic environment. When the objective is to address environmental problems beyond their borders, this should be done through regional or international agreement, not unilateral coercion.

The charge is made by some, however, that by discouraging the use of trade sanctions, the WTO constrains those concerned about global environmental problems from pursuing their goals. The Preamble to the Agreement Establishing the WTO talks of the desire for the "optimal use of the world's resources in accordance with the objective of sustainable development." It is argued that by not permitting unilateral action on the part of some countries to enforce standards or not formally authorizing multilateral action by countries taking trade measures under certain conditions, the WTO is an important player in the field of environmental policy. And by denying access to the WTO dispute settlement mechanism to enforce environmental standards beyond national borders, some say, environmentalists are blocked from using a powerful and effective tool to enforce standards that could have a direct effect on the global commons.

Most proposals to define the relationship of WTO rules to those of MEAs assume that, subject to specific conditions being met, certain trade measures taken pursuant to MEAs should benefit from special treatment under the WTO provisions.[31] This approach has been described as creating "an environmental window" in the WTO. The intention behind these proposals is to put in place whatever is necessary to avoid a dispute between conflicting obligations in an MEA and the WTO. This could be done, for example, through an amendment to one or more of the WTO agreements. There could be an amendment to the exceptions provisions: measures taken to protect the environment that would otherwise be inconsistent with the WTO could be automatically accepted if they were taken pursuant to an MEA that provided for such measures. In terms of the test of the "necessity" of discriminatory measures to fulfill an environmental objective, the interpretation of necessity would be determined by the existence of a broad-based MEA.

In pursuing such a course of action there would need to be some agreement on which MEAs were relevant for these purposes; a list would need to be drawn up, or at least the characteristics of the MEAs benefitting from this treatment would have to be defined. The criteria could be, for instance, that the negotiation of the MEA reflected a genuine international consensus. In providing some favored status in the WTO for MEAs, account would have to be taken of the fact that countries may not wish to join the MEA for a variety of reasons. As noted earlier, a country may find the scientific evidence unpersuasive, it may not be able to afford to join, or it may not have access to the necessary technology on favorable terms. It may not agree with a given environmental objective or with the means to achieve the objective, or it may consider there are more pressing national policy problems that deserve higher priority.

An alternative approach regarding measures taken pursuant to an MEA but in conflict with the WTO would be to decide after the event whether an exception should be granted for the measure in question. In special circumstances, for example, a waiver can be granted to a WTO obligation, subject to approval by at least three-quarters of WTO members. This could provide a measured, case-by-case response to any problems that might arise in the future. Evidence of a multilateral consensus would be established on the merits of each case, since it could be presumed that an MEA that could genuinely claim broad support from the international community would find equally broad support among WTO members.

Yet this approach has not received general support. A waived obligation is time-limited and must be renewed periodically; and a trade measure applied pursuant to a waiver could still be challenged in WTO dispute settlement on the grounds of nonviolation, nullification, and impairment of WTO rights. Some consider the strictness of these conditions to be appropriate for protecting the rights of WTO members in circumstances in which, for example, MEA parties apply WTO-inconsistent discriminatory trade measures against nonparties.

It has been proposed in the CTE, however, that the waiver approach could be modified to make it more attractive for environmental purposes. Provision could be made for a special "multiyear" waiver for trade measures applied pursuant to MEAs. All such measures taken under MEAs would be eligible for a waiver, provided they meet specified criteria, and a "negative vetting" approach could be adopted whereby the waiver would be automatically renewed if no new developments affect the exceptional circumstances that justified it in the first place. Specific trade measures contained in existing and future MEAs, whether among parties or against nonparties, could be granted a waiver on a case-by-case basis subject to nonbinding guidelines. The waiver would be extended annually until its termination as long as the WTO requirements are met, and the "exceptional circumstances" referred to in that provision would cover specific trade measures included in MEAs.

As waivers are voted on by WTO members, presumably there would be little resistance to a waiver being accepted if there were broad-based support for the MEA, as long as there was effective coordination between different parts of national administrations. Nevertheless, resort to any test of voting on a waiver in the WTO could fail to provide MEA negotiators with a necessary degree of security or predictability in their negotiations, and it might entail the WTO passing judgement over other international legal instruments. This could give rise to an untenable situation for WTO members that have accepted obligations under both the WTO and an MEA.

If a special status is assigned to measures taken pursuant to an "approved" MEA, the issue then is whether it is appropriate to provide for differentiated treatment for trade measures applied pursuant to the environmental agreement, depending on whether they apply between parties or against nonparties and whether the measures are specifically mandated in the MEA itself. The vagueness of the domestic measures provided for in the Kyoto Protocol provides an example.

A further issue, as noted in the discussion on climate change, is which dispute settlement system would deal with a conflict over a trade measure adopted for environmental purposes and in accordance with an MEA. As with the Dispute Settlement Understanding of the WTO, MEAs emphasize the avoidance of disputes. They include provisions to increase transparency through the collection and exchange of information, coordination of technical and scientific research, and collective monitoring of implementing measures, as well as consultation provisions. Most of the MEAs that are the focus of the CTE's work contain mechanisms for resolving disputes. These range from nonbinding, consensus-building mechanisms to binding, judicial procedures of arbitration, and in certain cases resort to the International Court of Justice.

It seems reasonable that an eventual dispute between WTO members who are parties to the MEA in the application of these measures should in the first instance be pursued under the dispute settlement procedures of the MEA. MEA parties might stipulate from the outset that they intend trade disputes arising out of implementation of the obligations of the MEA to be settled under the MEA's provisions. It could be argued that this approach can help ensure the convergence of the objectives of MEAs and the WTO while safeguarding their respective spheres of competence, thus overcoming problems arising from overlapping jurisdictions. It has been suggested that there may be value in strengthening MEA dispute settlement mechanisms, but of course this lies outside WTO jurisdiction.

It has been proposed in the CTE that measures applied among parties but not specifically mandated in any legal instrument relating to the environment, as well as those applied against nonparties that are specifically mandated in the legal instrument, could be tested through WTO dispute settlement against procedural and substantive criteria that would be set out in an "understanding" established by WTO members. The understanding would not apply to trade measures taken against nonparties to the instrument that were not specifically mandated by it; nor would it apply to unilateral measures. These would continue to be subject to existing WTO provisions.

It is increasingly apparent that it is in the interests of the WTO and environmentalists for environmental problems to be dealt with by those qualified to do so. The WTO is not an environmental policymaking institution. What this argues for is an approach in which new MEAs continue to be established—and existing ones strengthened—to deal with environmental problems of international concern. If there are grounds for discrimination in trade because of the characteristics of what is being traded (endangered species) or how a product is produced (carbon-emitting production processes), it could be argued that the solution lies with those with expertise to decide how to deal with the problem. If the agreed solution involves a loss of rights under the WTO (that is, being discriminated against), then providing all WTO members agree to forgo those rights, it is difficult to see where there could be a problem. Not surprisingly, WTO members as well as panel and appellate body reports have strongly promoted the use of multilateral or other environmental agreements to deal with problems relating to the environment.

NOTES

[1] For the text and discussion of the Communique, see Institute for Trade and Sustainable Development, "G7–G8 Endorse Trade-Environment Link," in *Bridges Between Trade and Sustainable Development*, Year 3, No. 5 (June 1999).

[2] The Committee was also charged under this heading to examine the relationship between environmental policies relevant to trade and environmental measures with significant trade effects and the provisions of the multilateral trading system.

[3] For a particularly comprehensive presentation of these and other proposals made in the Committee on Trade and Environment (CTE), see Kenneth P. Ewing and Richard D. Tarasofsky, *The Trade and Environment Agenda: Survey of Major Issues and Proposals, from Marrakesh to Singapore*, Environment Policy and Law Paper No. 33 (Gland, Switzerland: World Conservation Union–IUCN, 1997).

[4] The Montreal Protocol (1989 entry into force; 161 signatories) has as its intention the prevention of further depletion of the ozone layer, which protects the earth against ultraviolet rays. The protocol calls for signatory countries to ban, or phase out, the production of chlorofluorocarbons and other ozone-depleting substances. The signatories are prohibited from trading in these products with any country that has not signed the protocol unless that party can prove that it meets the environmental requirements of the protocol. See Donald M. Goldberg et al., *Effectiveness of Trade and Positive Measures in Multilateral Environmental Agreements: Lessons from the Montreal Protocol* (Washington, DC: CIEL, 1998).

The Convention on International Trade in Endangered Species of Wild Fauna and Flora (1975 entry into force; 132 signatories) is the oldest of the broad-based MEAs that uses trade measures to protect the environment. It bans trade in either live endangered species or the parts of dead ones; for a discussion, see Dale Andrews, *Experience with the Use of Trade Measures in CITES*, Joint Session of Trade and Environment Experts, OECD/GD(97)106 (Paris: OECD, 1997).

The Basel Convention on the Control of Transboundary Movement of Hazardous Wastes and Their Disposal (1992 entry into force; 113 signatories) imposes bans on the trade in hazardous wastes for final disposal between Organisation for Economic Co-operation and Development (OECD) and non-OECD countries; for a discussion, see Jonathan Krueger, *The Basel Convention and Transboundary Movements of Hazardous Wastes*, Briefing Paper No. 45 (London: Royal Institute of International Affairs, May 1998).

The Biosafety Protocol (under negotiation) has as its intention the creation of an advanced informed agreement procedure for importing or exporting living things that have been genetically modified.

[5] For a discussion of a variety of MEAs and WTO rules, see Robert Housman et al. (eds.), *The Use of Trade Measures in Select Environmental Agreements*, Environment and Trade Series No. 10 (Geneva, UNEP, 1995). See also Dale Andrews, *Trade Measures in Multilateral Environment Agreements: Synthesis Report of Three Case Studies*, COM/ENV/td, Joint Session of Trade and Environment Experts (Paris: OECD, 12 November 1998).

[6] See WTO, *Report on the Committee on Trade and Environment*, WT/CTE/W/1, Section 11, Item 1.12 (Geneva: WTO, November 1996).

[7] In the shrimp-turtle case, which dealt with fishing standards for shrimp, the appellate body found the United States to be in error with respect to its failure to enter into multilateral or bilateral talks with the complaining countries in order to conclude an agreement protecting sea turtles. (See also Chapter 7.) The United States did not enter into negotiations before imposing the import ban. The government did negotiate and conclude one regional agreement, the Inter-American Convention, which proved that alternative courses of action to the imposition of an embargo were available. In fact, the relevant U.S. legislation directs the Secretary of State to initiate negotiations, and these should have been attempted before imposing an embargo.

[8] This topic is also addressed comprehensively in Duncan Brack, *International Trade and Climate Change Policies* (London: Royal Institute of International Affairs, 1999).

[9] "The Parties should cooperate to promote a supportive and open international economic system that would lead to sustainable economic growth and development in all Parties, particularly developing country Parties, thus enabling them better to address the problems of climate change. Measures taken to combat climate change, including unilateral ones, should not con-

stitute a means of arbitrary or unjustifiable discrimination or a disguised restriction on international trade." (Article 3.5).

[10] Industrial countries commit themselves to reduce their collective emissions of six key greenhouse gases by at least 5 percent below 1990 levels. This group target will be achieved through cuts of 8 percent by Switzerland, most Central and East European states, and the European Union (which will meet its target by distributing different rates to its members states); 7 percent by the United States; and 6 percent by Canada, Hungary, Japan, and Poland. Russia, New Zealand, and Ukraine are to stabilize their emissions, while Norway may increase emissions by up to 1 percent, Australia by up to 8 percent, and Iceland 10 percent. The six gases are to be combined in a "basket," with reductions in individual gases translated into "carbon dioxide equivalents" that are then added up to produce a single figure. The European Union will, for example, be bound by a specific commitment to a reduction of 8 percent.

[11] See Kyoto Protocol, Article 2:1.

[12] Ibid., Article 2:3.

[13] Not surprisingly, the possibility of an eventual conflict between the rights and obligations of the WTO and what emerges from the future negotiations to address climate change concerns has been flagged by a number of authors. See Donald M. Goldberg, "The Framework Convention on Climate Change," in R. Housman et al. (eds.), *The Use of Trade Measures in Select Multilateral Environmental Agreements* (Geneva: UNEP and CIEL, 1995). See also Richard B. Stewart, Jonathan B. Wiener, and Philippe Sands, *Legal Issues Presented by a Pilot International Greenhouse Gas Trading System* (Geneva: UNCTAD, 1996).

[14] In this respect, Sir Leon Brittan, in his capacity as Vice President of the European Commission, recently expressed a balanced degree of concern: "Most of the governments that signed up to the Uruguay Round also accepted the outcome of Kyoto. There is a clear need for policy coherence here, and we owe it to ourselves to ensure that we do not make our task more difficult by taking on obligations that are incompatible." See Leon Brittan, in Saddrudin Aga Khan (ed.), *Policing the Global Economy: Why, How and For Whom* (London: Cameron and May, 1998).

[15] Article 2 of the Kyoto Protocol, for example, states that: "Each Party included in Annex 1, in achieving its quantified emission limitation and reduction commitments under Article 3, in order to promote sustainable development shall implement and /or further elaborate policies and measures in accordance with its national circumstances, such as: Enhancement of energy efficiency in relevant sectors . . . protection and enhancement of sinks . . . promotion of sustainable forms of agriculture . . . etc."

[16] See Goldberg, op. cit. note 13; see also Stewart, Wiener, and Sands, op. cit. note 13.

[17] Denmark, Finland, the Netherlands, Norway, and Sweden.

[18] See Richard Baron et al., *Economic/Fiscal Instruments: Taxation Working Paper 4, Policies and Measures for Common Action*, Annex I Expert Group on UNIFCCC, OECD/IEA (Paris: OECD, 1996), Section 3.2.2.3.

[19] From an efficiency perspective, it would be perverse for a government to rebate a tax to internalize an externality. In the case "United States—Taxes on Petroleum and Certain Imported Substances," the European Community argued that the tax imposed by the United

States on certain chemicals should not be eligible for border tax adjustment because it was designed to tax polluting activities that occurred in the United States. The panel concluded that the tax on certain chemicals, being a tax directly imposed on products, was eligible for border tax adjustment independent of the purpose it served. The panel therefore did not examine whether the tax on chemicals served environmental purposes and, if so, whether a border tax adjustment would be consistent with these purposes.

[20] In 1968, a Working Party on Border Tax Adjustments was established in the General Agreement on Tariffs and Trade (GATT) to examine the agreement's provisions relevant to border tax adjustments, the practices of contracting parties in relation to such adjustments, and their possible effects on international trade. The Working Party's report was adopted on 2 December 1970.

[21] For a comprehensive discussion, see WTO Secretariat, *Taxes and Charges for Environmental Purposes: Border Tax Adjustment*, WT/CTE/W/47 (Geneva: WTO, 2 May 1997).

[22] For a comprehensive discussion of this and related matters, see Frieder Roessler, "Diverging Domestic Policies and Multilateral Trade Integration," in Jagdish Bhagwati and Robert Hudec (eds.), *Fair Trade and Harmonisation: Prerequisites for Free Trade?* (Cambridge, MA: The MIT Press, 1996).

[23] Other such taxes include consumption taxes on capital equipment, auxiliary materials, and services used in the transportation and production of other taxable goods (such as taxes on advertising, energy, machinery, and transport).

[24] The view that taxes levied on non-product-related production methods are not eligible for adjustment has been challenged in the CTE on the grounds that GATT jurisprudence remains unclear on this point, and that certain important environmental taxes and charges might fall into the category of taxes on which the 1970 Working Party did not reach a firm conclusion. See WTO, *Report (1996) of the Committee on Trade and Environment*, Report of CTE to Singapore Ministerial Conference, WT/CTE/1 (Geneva: WTO, 12 November 1996).

[25] The 1970 Working Party noted that "there was a divergence of views with regard to the eligibility for adjustment of certain categories of tax," such as those that encompass consumption taxes on capital equipment, auxiliary materials, and services used in the transportation and production of other taxable goods, as well as taxes on advertising, energy, machinery, and transport. The Working Party did not investigate the matter, for it felt that while this area of taxation was unclear, its importance—as indicated by the scarcity of complaints reported in this connection—was not such as to justify further examination.

[26] These discussions relate primarily to the Agreement on Subsidies and Countervailing Measures (SCM), in particular its provisions on "Prohibited Subsidies" (Article 3 and Annex I) and its "Guidelines on Consumption of Inputs in the Production Process" (Annex II). WTO Secretariat, op. cit. note 21, also addresses the legitimacy of process-related subsidies.

[27] One view is that energy taxes appear to be covered by Footnote 61 of the SCM Agreement. Another is that the principle of physical incorporation remains the basis upon which border tax adjustment is applied.

[28] This point is taken up more comprehensively in Chapter 5.

[29] See World Wide Fund for Nature, *Climate Change and Compliance* (Gland, Switzerland: WWF, June 1998).

[30] According to the General Agreement on Trade in Services (GATS), a measure is defined in very broad terms: any measure by a member, whether in the form of a law, regulation, rule, procedure, decision, administrative action, or any other form. See Article XXXVIII (definitions) of the GATS.

[31] All the following proposals have been discussed at length in the CTE in one form or another.

A POWERFUL MECHANISM

■ THE DISPUTE SETTLEMENT PRACTICES of the World Trade Organization (WTO) as they emerged from the Uruguay Round built on 50 years of experience with the General Agreement on Tariffs and Trade (GATT). The current practices are inscribed in the Dispute Settlement Understanding (DSU), which is viewed by many as one of the most significant outcomes of the Uruguay Round and an effective way to promote multilateralism in the resolution of trade conflicts.[1] Despite this positive view, the dispute settlement process is one of the most criticized aspects of the work of the WTO.[2] The principal criticisms of the Dispute Settlement Body (DSB) fall under two categories. The first relates to process and lack of openness; a common criticism is that all hearings should be open to the public and that all briefs by the parties be made publicly available at the time of submission. The second is substance and relates to rulings that have been unpopular with environmentalists.

One reason for the chorus of criticism is that the process moves forward more automatically now than under GATT. This makes the lack of outside involvement even more aggravating. The automatic nature is evident, for example, in the decision-making process. In general, the DSB takes decisions by consensus, as is the case throughout the WTO. "Consensus" in other parts of the organization means no WTO member present at a meeting formally objects to the proposed decision.[3] But a radically different procedure is followed at four key stages in dispute settlement: establishment of a panel, adoption of a panel report, adoption of an appellate body report, and authorization for retaliation. At each stage, the decision is taken to accept the request or adopt the report unless there is a consensus *against* it.[4]

This rule of negative consensus makes decision-making quasi-automatic, in sharp contrast to the situation that prevailed under GATT 1947, when reports of panels could only be adopted on the basis of consensus. The DSU provides no opportunity for blockage in decision-making by the losing party, as frequently occurred under GATT.

Environmentalists and others are also concerned about the binding character of WTO obligations backed up by a compliance mechanism that provides for the payment of compensation and application of sanctions in the case of noncompliance. The "losing" member in a dispute is expected to implement panel or appellate body recommendations, and there are incentives for doing so. If the government concerned fails within a reasonable period to follow the recommended course of action, the parties may agree to compensation. Without such an agreement, the "winning" member may retaliate after obtaining DSB authorization. As a general principle the complaining party should first seek to suspend concessions or other obligations in the sector in which the breach of obligation has occurred, but retaliation can also be taken under any other agreement. (See Chapter 2.)

In this chapter I do not describe all aspects of the dispute settlement process in the WTO. This has been done at length in other excellent tomes.[5] I do, however, describe the aspects that are the most criticized and conclude with some proposed changes and their implications.

. . . .

THE DISPUTE SETTLEMENT PROCESS

■ ANY MEMBER OF THE WTO THAT BELIEVES benefits accruing to it under a WTO Agreement are being impaired by measures taken by another member can invoke the dispute settlement system. In most cases, a WTO member will claim that a measure enacted by another member violates one or more of the substantive provisions contained in a WTO agreement. The DSU is applicable in a uniform manner to all disputes under any WTO agreement.[6] WTO dispute settlement is not open to WTO observers, other international organizations, nongovernmental organizations (NGOs), local governments, or private persons. The mechanism is essentially an intergovernmental forum, with private parties being represented by their respective governments, though a panel may consult with any entity or person if it so wishes.

The DSU contains rules and procedures on both consultations and adjudication.[7] It favors solutions mutually acceptable to the parties to the dispute, provided they are consistent with WTO agreements. In the absence of a mutually agreed solution, the ultimate objective of the dispute settlement mechanism is to secure the withdrawal of the measures concerned if they are found to be inconsistent with WTO agreements. If this cannot be achieved, the dispute will be adjudicated by panels composed of experts convened on an ad hoc basis. Panel reports may be subject to appeal to the appellate body, a permanent group of seven experts in trade issues and trade law who are in charge of reviewing the legal aspects of reports issued by panels. (See Box 7–1 for an overview of the various components of the dispute settlement system.)

All WTO members are entitled to participate in the Dispute Settlement Body. This group's primary tasks are to supervise the functioning of dispute resolution under the WTO and, in particular, to establish dispute settlement panels, to adopt reports from panels or the appellate body, and to authorize suspension of concessions and retaliation by one party if another party fails to implement the conclusions of a report.

When a panel or the appellate body concludes that a measure is inconsistent with a covered argument, it must recommend that the member concerned bring the measure into conformity with that agreement. In addition, the panel or appellate body may suggest ways in which the member concerned could implement the recommendations.

· ·

DE FACTO
RULE-MAKING

■ ALTHOUGH THE RULES OF THE GATT HAVE rarely been changed, some flexibility exists for taking measures that would under normal circumstances be considered violations of WTO rules. As described in Chapter 6, nonconforming measures can be taken for environmental purposes if they are necessary to protect human, animal, or plant life or health, or if they relate to the conservation of exhaustible natural resources and are made effective in conjunction with restrictions on domestic production or consumption.[8] If these conditions are fulfilled, then the remaining requirement is that they not be applied in an arbitrary or unjustifiable manner so as to discriminate between countries where the same conditions prevail. They are not to be disguised restrictions on international trade.[9]

This raises some basic questions: Why is an exception necessary at all if national measures are applied to imports? Are not WTO members free to adopt whatever measures they wish to implement their national policy

CONSULTATION

■ Members agree to give sympathetic consideration to and adequate opportunity for consultation regarding any representation made by another member concerning measures affecting the operation of any WTO agreement.

■ Director-General may offer good offices, conciliation, or mediation to help settle a dispute; this may continue while panel process gets under way.

PANEL

■ Complaining party may ask DSB to establish a panel to review factual and legal aspects of case if no settlement is reached within 60 days of request for consultations.

■ Panel members, usually acting or former trade diplomats, serve in individual capacities.

■ Panel receives written submissions from main parties and any other WTO member that has a "substantial interest" in the case; at least two hearings are held for oral arguments and questions by the panel.

■ Parties to the dispute can comment on both the draft descriptive report and an interim full report.

■ Panels may set up expert review groups on scientific or technical matters; members of these serve in individual capacities and may not include government officials of any parties to the dispute.

■ Final report must be issued within six months of agreement on composition and terms of reference of panel.

■ Reports are generally unrestricted at the same time as they are circulated to all WTO members.

■ Report must be adopted within 60 days of circulation to all members unless a party to the dispute notifies DSB of intent to appeal; DSB cannot consider a report that is being appealed.

APPEAL

■ Appellate body is a standing group of seven experts appointed by DSB for four-year terms; each member may be reappointed once.

■ Appellate body must generally complete its review within 60 days; in no case shall the review exceed 90 days.

■ Appeals are limited to issues of law covered in the panel report and legal interpretations developed by the panel.

■ Appellate body may uphold, modify, or reverse the legal findings and conclusions of a panel.

■ Appellate body is not allowed to add or subtract any rights and obligations of members provided in the covered agreements.

■ Within 30 days of its circulation to members, appellate body report must be adopted by DSB and accepted by parties to the dispute unless DSB decides otherwise by consensus.

Source: Box derives from the "Understanding on Rules and Procedures Governing the Settlement of Disputes," in The Results of the Uruguay Round of Multilateral Trade Negotiations: The Legal Text *(Geneva: WTO, 1995).*

choices with respect to the environment? Indeed, the national treatment provision of the WTO requires governments to apply the same regulations to imported and domestically produced products. But as described in Chapter 6, these regulations apply only to the product and not the process of production. The interpretation of like product in the national treatment provision, however, is just that—a matter of interpretation. For measures to be WTO-consistent, products with the same physical form are to be considered to be like products by the importing country, irrespective of whether they have been produced in an environmentally friendly manner. The possibility of imposing WTO-inconsistent measures is, however, provided for in the exceptions provisions of the GATT.

Yet measures taken as exceptions have often been challenged through the dispute settlement process. Under GATT, six panel proceedings involving an examination of environmental measures or human health-related measures under the exceptions provisions were completed; out of the six reports, three remained unadopted. So far, two such proceedings have been completed under the WTO's DSU.

The reading of these exceptions by the panels has been narrow, and none of the exception measures taken for environmental purposes has been successfully defended. Not surprisingly, the interpretation of the exceptions provision by WTO trade officials is a source of friction with environmentalists. In this respect, two points are important. First, none of the panels has in any way questioned the environmental policy choices underlying the national measures at issue. Second, of the 450 plus requests for consultation under the dispute settlement process of GATT and the WTO in the past half-century, only eight panels have been established that could be considered to be environment-related. (A brief description of the relevant facts of each case is provided in the Appendix to this essay.)

A great deal has been written on how the exceptions provision has been interpreted in these eight cases.[10] The intention here is not to discuss the cases per se; interested readers can consult a large body of literature on this.[11] In addition, this chapter cannot address all issues; rather, it provides examples of contentious interpretations of rules. The policy implication is that there is a pressing need for discussion of the policy choices open to WTO members rather than interpretation through inconclusive litigation. To the extent possible, only the shrimp-turtle dispute will be considered here. [In this case, four countries complained about a U.S. ban on imports of shrimp (and shrimp products) caught by trawlers that do not use a special device in their nets to protect five species of sea turtles from being caught inadvertently; see the Appendix for details.]

As indicated in the discussion of multilateral environmental agreements in Chapter 6, one of the most contentious issues is whether WTO members can, under the GATT exceptions provisions, take otherwise nonconforming measures to protect the environment not only in their own countries but also in the global commons or in their trading partners. Can WTO obligations be breached to ensure that certain standards deemed appropriate by the importing country are applied in the exporting country as a precondition for doing business? From the perspective of environmentalists, having access to an effective means to ensure the extraterritorial application of minimum standards is a key issue.

Whether this is permissible is not formally established by the text of the GATT exceptions provision itself. It is a matter for interpretation by panels and the appellate body. Much to the chagrin of many environmentalists, the traditional interpretation has been that trade measures relating to environmental standards should be taken only with respect to the fauna and flora and natural resources within the boundaries of the country taking the action.[12] The implications are clear. Countries are free to adopt whatever regulations they wish to reflect standards within their own borders, but they cannot restrict trade on the grounds that other countries do not apply these standards domestically. In practical terms, this means that while a country may adopt whatever fishing practices for tuna or shrimp it wishes to protect dolphins, turtles, or any other sea life, it cannot refuse to import tuna or shrimp from countries that choose not to adopt the same or equivalent standards.

This approach has, however, been called into question by a recent appellate body ruling in the shrimp-turtle dispute.[13] The appellate body ruled against the measure taken by the United States to restrict imported shrimp on the grounds that it was applied "in a manner which amounts to a means not just of unjustifiable discrimination, but also of 'arbitrary' discrimination between countries where the same conditions prevail." This, it was concluded, was contrary to the requirements of the heading of the GATT exceptions article; the U.S. measure was not entitled to the justifying protection of the exceptions article of the GATT 1994.[14] But the important question left open is what would happen if the United States met the requirements of the appellate body and applied its standards extraterritorially but in a nondiscriminatory manner.

The United States disagreed with the appellate body ruling that it had applied its law in an arbitrary and unjustifiable manner, but it could agree to the adoption of the report as it made a "number of important findings that helped clarify the critical relationship between the WTO rules and measures taken to protect the environment." Most important, it is

> of considerable significance that the appellate body had not accepted the complainants' argument that some sort of jurisdictional limitations would prevent the use of Article XX(g) with respect to the measures in question. The United States was pleased that the appellate body had emphasized that Article XX had to be "read by a treaty interpreter in light of contemporary concerns of the community of nations about the protection and conservation of the environment."[15]

Not surprisingly, others view this decision with dismay. The view of Thailand, for example, was shared by others:

> This decision permitted Members to discriminate against products based on non-product related processes and production methods (PPMs). This was a fundamental and impermissible alteration of the present balance of the rights and obligations of Members under the WTO Agreement. . . . The right to discriminate based on like products had not been negotiated in the Uruguay Round. The appellate body, upon its own will, had altered the balance of rights and obligations under the WTO Agreement.[16]

In the view of India, if "the present decision of the appellate body were deemed applicable to all future measures, then the door would open to unilateral measures aimed at discrimination based on non-product-related PPMs."[17]

Notwithstanding the ostensible change in approach to the application of unilateral measures, the appellate body appeared to support the panel finding when it examined whether measures "necessary to protect the life and health of animals could include measures taken so as to force other countries to change their policies within their own jurisdiction, and requiring such changes in order to be effective." The panel concluded that such measures, which would be effective only with policy changes in other countries, could not be considered "necessary" within the meaning of Article XX(b).[18] In the view of the appellate body, "[p]erhaps the most conspicuous flaw in this measure's application related to its intended and actual coercive effect on the specific policy decisions made by foreign governments, Members of the WTO."[19] It considered that

> it is not acceptable, in international trade relations, for one WTO Member to use an economic embargo to require other Members to adopt essentially the same comprehensive regulatory program, to achieve a certain policy goal, as that in force within that Member's territory, without taking into consideration different conditions which may occur in the territories of those other Members.[20]

So although, as noted earlier, the appellate body did not directly address the question of the acceptability of extraterritorial action, it is difficult to see how this ruling sits with the belief of some (see the U.S. statement) that had the U.S. measure been applied in a nonarbitrary and justifiable manner, it would have been deemed acceptable to the appellate body.

Perhaps rulings such as this have some short-term merit in finding immediate "solutions" to politically sensitive matters, but in the long term, policy choices as important as the legitimacy of the unilateral application of trade measures to enforce domestic societal preferences extraterritorially should not be left to litigation of this nature, with confusing and uncertain outcomes. These should be the subject of policy debates with the participation of representatives from all WTO members.

A further issue thrown into confusion through the dispute resolution process is the status of the preamble in GATT and WTO agreements. Is the text there only hortatory, or can it have legal meaning? This problem became apparent in the decision on whether the term "renewable resources" [as in Article XX(g)] applied to renewable biological resources or was limited to depletable mineral resources. In the shrimp-turtle case, the appellate body noted that U.S. shrimp-turtle law, by encouraging exporting countries to adopt sea turtle conservation programs, was directly connected with the policy of sea turtle conservation, and thus was a measure "relating" to conservation, and that GATT exceptions were not limited to the conservation of "mineral" or "non-living" natural resources. According to the appellate body, living species, which are in principle renewable, "are in certain circumstances indeed susceptible of depletion, exhaustion and extinction, frequently because of human activities."[21]

This view was based in large measure on the importance assigned by the appellate body to the Preamble to the Agreement Establishing the WTO, and its content when compared with the GATT.[22] The WTO preamble is, according to the appellate body, to give "colour, texture and shading to the rights and obligations of Members under the WTO Agreement." The appellate body noted that "given the recent acknowledgement by the international community of the importance of concerted bilateral or multilateral action to protect living natural resources, and recalling the explicit recognition by WTO Members of the objective of sustainable development in the preamble of the WTO Agreement, we believe it is too late in the day to suppose that Article XX(g) of the GATT 1994 may be read as referring only to the conservation of exhaustible mineral or other non-living natural resources."[23] In taking responsibility for this "coloring in" exercise, the appellate body certainly assigned a great deal of responsibility to itself in this and future cases.

Further, as "all of the seven recognised species of sea turtles are listed in Appendix 1 of the Convention on International Trade in Endangered Species of Wild Fauna and Flora," the appellate body concluded that the five species of sea turtles involved in the dispute constitute "exhaustible natural resources" within the meaning of Article XX(g) of the GATT 1994.[24] It asserted that "we have not decided that the sovereign nations that are Members of the WTO cannot adopt effective measures to protect endangered species, such as sea turtles. Clearly, they can and should." The appellate body held further that "WTO Members are free to adopt their own policies aimed at protecting the environment as long as, in doing so, they fulfil their obligations and respect the rights of other Members under the WTO Agreement."

Principles as expressed in preambles are general legal commitments rather than specific legal obligations of states.[25] In making a ruling to the contrary, the appellate body clearly assigned importance to promoting sustainable development and preserving the environment, something that appears only in the preamble. This objective is certainly recognized and supported by WTO members. The manner in which it is translated into rights and obligations can fundamentally change the character of the exceptions provisions of the WTO. Indeed, a number of WTO members believe that it rendered inoperable one of the principal paragraphs of the exceptions provisions.

. . . .

AMICUS BRIEFS

■ ANOTHER IMPORTANT QUESTION IS WHETHER a panel or the appellate body is obliged to accept information submitted in the form of amicus briefs by NGOs.[26] This became a particular issue in the shrimp-turtle case, in which three submissions were received from NGOs, all with expertise in turtle conservation.[27] The defending country, the United States, argued that nothing in the DSU prohibits panels from considering information just because it was unsolicited. The language of the DSU is broadly drafted, it was argued, to provide a panel with discretion in choosing its sources of information. It can "seek" such information from whomever it pleases. The United States argued that to find otherwise would unnecessarily limit the discretion that the DSU affords panels in choosing the sources of information to consider.

The panel found that it could not accept nonrequested submissions from NGOs, as this would be incompatible with the DSU provisions. It explained that the initiative to seek information and to select the source of information rested with the panel alone, and noted that only the parties to the dispute and third parties could submit information directly to panels. The appellate body, however, ruled that "the Panel erred in its legal interpretations that accepting non-requested information from non-governmental sources is incompatible with the provisions of the DSU."[28]

The complaining countries objected to the appellate body's ruling, arguing that this procedure was not in conformity with the working procedures. The briefs represent the views of NGOs rather than the United States, and this gives rise to contradictions, internal inconsistencies, and serious procedural and systemic problems. As the briefs were attached to the U.S. submission, it was unclear if they were part of the U.S. argumentation. The appellate body asked the United States to what extent it agreed with the legal arguments set out in the briefs appended to its submission. The government stated that it was not adopting these views as separate matters to which the appellate body had to respond, and that it agreed with the legal arguments in the NGO submissions to the extent that those arguments concurred with arguments set out in its main submission.

Further, the complaining parties argued, as members that are not parties or third parties cannot avail themselves of the right to present written submissions, it would be unreasonable to grant the right to submit an unsolicited written submission to a nonmember when many members do not enjoy a similar right. Such information might be strongly biased if nationals from members involved in a dispute could provide unsolicited information. The complaining parties reasoned that this would only increase the administrative tasks of the already overburdened Secretariat. They also reasoned that the parties to a dispute might feel obliged to respond to all unsolicited submissions, just in case one of the unsolicited submissions catches the attention of a panel member. Due process requires that a party know what submissions a panel intends to consider, and that all parties be given an opportunity to respond to all submissions.

For many countries, once again, the most important consideration in this issue is a systemic one. In its ruling, had the appellate body taken into consideration more than the issues of law and legal interpretation? In the view of some, by ruling against the appellees, the appellate body had given NGOs the right to make submissions that had exceeded the rights of members not participating in this dispute. Thus the appellate body had diminished the rights of members and intruded upon members' prerogative as negotiators to establish the bounds of participation in the WTO. Such issues should be decided by members. The appellate body, which was only a judiciary, was in this case writing the rules of participation.[29] At the time of the adoption of the shrimp-turtle appellate body report, it was argued that the DSU did not give NGOs the right to submit amicus briefs, nor did it permit members to attach briefs to their submissions that did not reflect their views. With regard to amicus briefs, the appellate body had appeared to have "let itself be overawed by the campaign of NGOs of major trading entities."[30]

. . . .

PRESERVING
THE SYSTEM?

■   DISPUTE SETTLEMENT CAN EVEN GIVE RISE to as fundamental a question as how much importance to give to the preservation of the multilateral trading system when it appears to be under threat. The shrimp-turtle panel noted that "by its very nature, the WTO Agreement favours a multilateral approach to trade issues," as shown in the Preamble to the WTO Agreement and the Dispute Settlement Understanding. On this basis, the panel concluded that the GATT exceptions option only allows members to derogate from GATT provisions so long as, in doing so, they do not undermine the WTO multilateral trading system.[31] The appellate body disagreed with the approach chosen by the panel in this respect: "Maintaining, rather than undermining, the multilateral trading system is necessarily a fundamental and pervasive premise underlying the WTO Agreement; but it is not a right or an obligation, nor is it an interpretative rule which can be employed in the appraisal of a given measure under the chapeau of Article XX."[32]

The appellate body pointed out that the role of the introductory text (or the chapeau) to Article XX was not to extend the rights or obligations of members. Thus,

> the task of interpreting and applying the chapeau is . . . essentially the delicate one of locating and marking out a line of equilibrium between the right of a Member to invoke an exception under Article XX and the rights of the other Members under varying substantive provisions (e.g., Article XI) of the GATT 1994. . . . The location of the line of equilibrium, as expressed in the chapeau, is not fixed and unchanging; the line moves as the kind and the shape of the measures at stake vary and as the facts making up specific cases differ.[33]

That "maintaining, rather than undermining, the multilateral trading system is necessarily a fundamental and pervasive premise underlying the WTO Agreement" is the view of a number of WTO Members. Thailand, for example, brought the shrimp-turtle dispute to the WTO

> not so much for its economic interest, but as a matter which involved a fundamental principle of the multilateral trading system . . . the application of unilateral and extraterritorial measures was unacceptable and incompatible with the multilateral trading system . . . a delicate balance of rights and obligations among Members, could be undermined and weakened by such measures. Under the multilateral trading system, no country could impose unilaterally its trade policies on other trading partners through a restrictive embargo.[34]

It is not clear how many countries would have joined the WTO had the concepts of "like product" and product- and non-product-related production processes been interpreted differently.

With regard to procedural issues, it has been argued by some members that the appellate body has extended its authority beyond that granted to it under the WTO Agreement. The DSU limited the jurisdiction of the appellate body to issues of law covered in panel reports and to legal interpretations developed by panels, and prohibited the appellate body from adding to or diminishing the rights and obligations provided in the covered agreements. A number of countries have argued that there has been an "evolutionary" interpretative approach adopted by the appellate body that has given a new interpretation to certain DSU provisions and overstepped the bounds of its authority by undermining the balance of rights and obligations of members.[35]

TRANSPARENCY

■   THERE HAVE BEEN A NUMBER OF PROPOSALS to make the dispute settlement process more open to public scrutiny. The current procedures are that there are closed meetings between the panelists and the parties. These are not open to third parties or to other WTO members. Third parties can make submissions to the panels—of course, along with the parties—but other WTO members cannot. There are hearings of the panel where third parties, but not other WTO members, can present their views.

The common elements of proposals for greater transparency in the dispute settlement process normally contain initiatives to formalize the acceptance of amicus briefs, open the proceedings of the panels, and receive the submissions of the parties when they are made available to the panel. (The accelerated distribution of panel reports is addressed in Chapter 3.) In the view of some, the arguments in favor of increased participation by NGOs in the dispute settlement process have been described as "overwhelming."[36] This is not the view of the majority of WTO members, however.

Indeed, there will be resistance to the adoption of the proposals of President Clinton and others. At the most fundamental level, governments will argue that the WTO is an intergovernmental organization and that governments should represent the collectivity of their constituents. It will also be argued that to have a public discussion of the national submissions at the same time as they are under discussion in the panel—with the possibility of that discussion influencing the panelists—could jeopardize the case of the parties. This formula could also conjure up visions of what has been described as "scorched earth" tactics, where defendants would use every technical objection available to create serious obstacles for the panel to adjudicate the dispute seriously.[37]

The stark reality is that under the pressure of domestic pressure groups, particularly in industrial countries, there will most probably be an opening up of the dispute settlement process to the public. It may well take time, as most WTO members (particularly developing countries) believe that this will not "enrich" the process when submissions are presented. The balanced approach is this, as noted by Robert Hudec: "While the proposal to allow public access to documents and hearings could well have a negative impact on party behavior, such public access would help to deflect serious attacks on the legitimacy of WTO legal rulings."[38] Notwithstanding the various reservations mentioned, there should be and will be an opening up of the WTO dispute settlement process. But it will take time.

In determining a time horizon for change in dispute processes, it is important to consider the different groups that are interested in the outcome of a dispute and their access to the process under current procedures. At least five groups are involved, including the parties to the dispute, the third parties that have a formal role to play in the dispute (that is, in accordance with the DSU), WTO members interested in the outcome of the dispute (perhaps from a systemic perspective), and NGOs (civil society). The fifth group has a very direct interest and is certainly the largest in terms of numbers. It consists of producers in both countries, producers in other competing countries, and consumers in all countries. It is clear from the discussions in the review of the DSU that governments will not permit more rights to be given to NGOs and other groups than they themselves have. A practical reality is that before the dispute process is made more publicly accessible, governments will have to decide on how they themselves are to be treated in this process. Given the consensus-based nature of the WTO, this will not happen quickly.

NOTES

[1] See Article 3.2 DSU. This multilateral system is based on the principles for the management of disputes developed under Articles XXII and XXIII of GATT 1947, as further elaborated and modified by the Dispute Settlement Understanding (DSU) (Article 3.1 DSU).

[2] See World Wide Fund for Nature, "Dispute Settlement in the WTO: A Crisis for Sustainable Development," Discussion Paper (Gland, Switzerland: WWF, May 1998).

[3] See footnote 1 to Article 2.4 DSU.

[4] For instance, the establishment of a panel is now automatic at the second meeting where it is requested; the adoption of panel and appellate body reports is also automatic; retaliation, too, is automatic if requested by the "winning" party.

[5] See, in particular, WTO Secretariat, *Analytical Index* (Geneva: WTO, 1995). See also Ernst-Ulrich Petersmann, *The GATT/WTO Dispute Settlement System: International Law, International Organisations and Dispute Settlement* (London: Kluwer Law International, 1996); Robert E. Hudec, "The New WTO Dispute Settlement Procedure: An Overview of the First Three Years," *Minnesota Journal of Global Trade,* Winter 1999; James Cameron and Karen Campbell (eds.), *Dispute Resolution in the World Trade Organisation* (London: Cameron and May, 1998).

[6] There are, however, special or additional rules contained in some specific WTO agreements. See WTO Secretariat, *The WTO Dispute Settlement Procedures—a Collection of the Legal Texts* (Geneva: WTO,1995).

[7] The WTO dispute settlement mechanism provides for three main ways of resolving disputes: bilateral consultations; good offices, conciliation, and mediation; and adjudication by a third entity, including arbitration. With the exception of arbitration, adjudication cannot be requested until consultations have taken place or unsuccessful attempts to consult have been made.

[8] The exceptions provisions for trade in services are very similar to those for trade in goods. Negotiated during the Uruguay Round, the General Agreement on Trade in Services (GATS) contains a General Exceptions clause in Article XIV, which starts with a chapeau identical to that of GATT Article XX. In addressing environmental concerns, GATS Article XIV(b) allows WTO members to adopt GATS-inconsistent policy measures if this is "necessary to protect human, animal or plant life or health" (and is identical to GATT Article XX (b)).

[9] See Headnote to Article XX.

[10] For exceptions cases in general, see WTO, op. cit. note 5.

[11] For a comprehensive study documenting all the Article XX environment cases in the GATT and the WTO—which puts a finer edge on all the legal considerations raised in the text—see WTO Secretariat, *GATT/WTO Dispute Settlement Practice relating to Article XX, Paragraphs (b), (d) and (g) of GATT*, WTO/CTE/W/53/Rev.1, 26 October 1998.

[12] While there has been flexibility in the WTO with respect to extraterritoriality, this has been circumscribed by the requirement that the objective of the measure is not to change the policy toward the environment in the exporting country. This, however, is the very purpose of most environmental measures of this nature.

[13] The question of whether Article XX(b) can be invoked to protect the life or health of animals outside the jurisdiction of the country invoking it was examined in the two tuna panel reports (see Appendix in this volume). The reasoning followed by the two panels differs on several points. In Tuna II, the panel found that "the policy to protect the life and health of dolphins in the eastern tropical Pacific Ocean, which the United States pursued within its jurisdiction over its nationals and vessels, fell within the range of policies covered by Article XX(b)." See Tuna I, paragraph 5.27 and Tuna II, paragraphs 5.31 to 5.33.

[14] Ibid., paragraphs 178–84.

[15] See WTO, *Minutes of Meeting of the Dispute Settlement Body*, WT/DSB/M/50, 14 December 1998, p. 11.

[16] Ibid., p. 4.

[17] Ibid., p. 10.

[18] This conclusion was justified as follows: "If Article XX(b) were interpreted to permit contracting parties to deviate from the basic obligations of the General Agreement by taking trade measures to implement policies within their own jurisdiction, including policies to protect living things, the objectives of the General Agreement would be maintained. If however Article XX(b) were interpreted to permit contracting parties to impose trade embargoes so

as to force other countries to change their policies within their jurisdiction, including policies to protect living things, and which required such changes to be effective, the objectives of the General Agreement would be seriously impaired." Tuna II, paragraphs 5.37 to 5.39.

[19] Appellate Body Report, *United States—Import Prohibition of Certain Shrimp and Shrimp Products*, WT/DS58/AB/R, paragraph 161.

[20] Ibid., paragraph 164.

[21] Shrimp Turtle Appellate Body Report, paragraph 128.

[22] Unlike the preamble to the GATT, the Preamble to the Agreement Establishing the World Trade Organization conditions WTO members in conducting their relations in the field of trade and economic endeavor "while allowing for the optimal use of the world's resources in accordance with the objective of sustainable development, seeking both to protect and preserve the environment and to enhance the means for doing so in a manner consistent with their respective needs and concerns at different levels of economic development."

[23] The appellate body continued that "Moreover, two adopted GATT 1947 panel reports previously found fish to be an 'exhaustible natural resource' within the meaning of Article XX(g) [reference to Tuna 1982 and Salmon/Herring]. We hold that, in line with the principle of effectiveness in treaty interpretation, measures to conserve exhaustible natural resources, whether living or non-living, may fall within Article XX(g)." Ibid., paragraphs 127–34.

[24] Ibid.

[25] Phillipe Sands, "International Law in the Field of Sustainable Development: Emerging Legal Principles," in Wilfred Lang (ed.), *Sustainable Development* (Netherlands: Kluwer Law International, 1995).

[26] At the celebrations to commemorate the Fiftieth Anniversary of the Multilateral Trading System, President Clinton lamented the fact that there is no mechanism for private citizens to provide input into WTO disputes. In concrete terms he proposed that the "WTO provide the opportunity for stakeholders to convey their views, such as the ability to file 'amicus briefs,' to help inform the panels in their deliberations."

[27] During the panel proceedings, the panel received briefs from the Center for Marine Conservation, the Center for International Environmental Law (CIEL), and the World Wild Fund for Nature, with copies to the complainants. During the appellate body proceedings, the United States attached to its submission amicus briefs from three groups of nongovernmental organizations (NGOs) (paragraph 79 of the Appellate Body Report). In addition, CIEL sent a revised version of its brief directly to the appellate body.

[28] See Appellate Body Report, paragraph 110.

[29] See the views of members as reported in WTO, op. cit. note 15, p. 11.

[30] Ibid, p. 10.

[31] Ibid., paragraph 7.43–7.44.

[32] The context was the appellate body criticism that the panel failed to scrutinize the immediate context of the chapeau paragraphs (a) to (j) of Article XX. Moreover, the panel did not look into the object and purpose of the chapeau of Article XX. Rather, it looked into the object and

purpose of the whole of the GATT 1994 and the WTO Agreement, which it described in an overly broad manner. Thus the Panel arrived at the very broad formulation that measures that "undermine the WTO multilateral trading system" [footnote omitted] must be regarded as "not within the scope of measures permitted under the chapeau of Article XX." See the Shrimp Appellate Body Report, paragraph 116.

[33] Ibid., paragraph 159.

[34] WTO, op. cit. note 15, p. 1.

[35] See comments by Malaysia, India, Pakistan, and others in WTO, op. cit. note 15.

[36] "Permitting NGOs to watch the proceedings when parties give evidence to dispute panels and to have access to written submissions would go a considerable distance toward dispelling fears about the unexplained 'black box' that hides WTO decisions emanating from the shores of Lake Geneva"; see Dan Esty, "Non Governmental Organisations at the World Trade Organisation: Cooperation, Competition, or Exclusion," *Journal of International Economic Law*, Vol. 1, No. 1 (March 1998), p. 144.

[37] See Hudec, op. cit., note 5.

[38] Ibid.

Chapter 8
Policy
Recommendations

THE POLITICS
OF WTO REFORM

■ IN THIS FINAL CHAPTER, I DRAW TOGETHER the policy recommendations that emerge from the earlier chapters. Some are in the form of proposals; others assign a priority to questions to be addressed in forthcoming negotiations. Most are general in nature, and some of the more specific or technical proposals can be found in the earlier chapters. The intention here is to take into account the substance as well as the political and institutional realities of the post-Seattle trade policy environment to offer workable and realistic proposals.

I start from the premise that any proposals involving a change in rights and obligations of World Trade Organization (WTO) members will be much more difficult to secure—and will take much longer—than those that can be achieved without such changes. Thus an important question is to what extent can the concerns of environmental nongovernmental organizations (NGOs) be met without changing rules, rights, and obligations in the WTO. In adopting this approach, the intention is not to trivialize the concerns of the environmental community, for much can be achieved without changing the rules and engaging in the concomitant negotiations between governments. In any event, proposals that do not require rule change can always be considered a first step, with initiatives to change the rules being pursued simultaneously or at later stages.

Numerous other practical considerations must be taken into account if proposals are to be realistic. Many trade officials—as represented in their national negotiating positions—will resist change, for they believe that the rules-based multilateral trading system works well as it is, with many of its rules and procedures still new and untried after the Uruguay Round. For them, changing the rules is not timely and brings risk—a risk not worth taking. WTO members have signed on to various agreements because they consider that overall there is a balance of rights and obligations that is acceptable from a national perspective. Upsetting this balance would require renegotiation of the agreements.

One dramatic example of this phenomenon comes from posing the question of how many governments would have joined the WTO if the concept of "like products" or "product and non-product-related production processes" had been interpreted in a way that allows trade sanctions to be applied according to the manner in which goods were produced. Would China show any interest at all in joining the WTO if its products could be discriminated against according to production methods? Would nondiscriminatory treatment in the WTO be linked to labor standards or even human rights?

Many developing countries also wonder why they should concede to the concerns of industrial countries to meet the demands of powerful NGOs. Developing countries can see that industrial countries, partly at the urging of domestic interest groups, wish to change the rules of the game, and in their view this carries considerable risk. From a negotiating perspective, developing countries will naturally seek to extract concessions from those looking for change. Also, some developing countries ask why they should go along with new negotiations when the commitments of industrial nations in the last round have not yet been implemented. If the "cost" is a failure to launch a new round of negotiations (or no fast-track authority in the United States), then not accommodating NGO demands only strengthens the negotiating position of the countries seeking implementation of existing commitments before launching into others in new negotiations. In addition, developing countries are suspicious of any efforts by environmental NGOs to use trade sanctions as a means to enforce production-related environmental standards. They believe it is merely a sideways step into similar regulations of labor standards. And in any event, the reasoning continues, even NGO initiatives driven by genuine concerns about the environment will surely fall captive to protectionist interests.

A further consideration is that views understandably differ among environmental groups, as they have diverse interests that translate into different priorities. In this sense, at least, there are clear parallels with different positions taken by national governments; they, too, have different priorities that reflect, for example, their trading interests, negotiating strategies, and levels of economic development. In some areas, such as the acceptability of unilateral action to enforce environmental standards, some NGOs will side more with the United States and the European Union; others—sympathizing with developing countries—will staunchly oppose such measures. Thus introducing change to accommodate the priorities and concerns of all—WTO members and environmental NGOs—will not be easy.

The WTO is above all a negotiating body where consensus is sought. This has important implications for the adoption of proposals. Trade-offs can be made and assurances granted in numerous ways. The fact that one country—or group of countries—is making a proposal means by definition that something is being sought from others, and potentially a price has to be paid for that. Good negotiators rarely give concessions to negotiating partners without extracting some return payment. It is important to know what to ask for. There is some optimism to be had in the thought that the WTO does not lack flexibility when it comes to finding the middle ground or an acceptable balance of rights and obligations. The approach in the proposals given here is an optimistic one—namely that in the aftermath of Seattle, the path to the middle ground can be found in the trade and environment debate by making the necessary trade-offs.

. . . .

INTERESTS OF DEVELOPING COUNTRIES

■ MORE THAN 100 OF THE WTO MEMBERS are developing countries. Their interests cannot be neglected in an organization where decisions are taken by consensus. Many of the trade-and-environment-related proposals put forward in the past have been of little if any interest to these nations. In fact, in many instances, they have lacked sensitivity to their needs; they frequently do not pay due regard to core principles such as common but differentiated responsibility, the right to development, or even the right to basic human needs such as food, health, and education that industrial countries take for granted.[1]

Because many developing countries consider the trade and environment debate to be a damage-limitation exercise, the post-Seattle agenda must contain a sufficient number of their priorities in other areas to engage developing countries fully in a debate. Trade-offs will be required for developing countries to agree to change, and countries seeking change have to be prepared to pay the "price." It is important to establish what the "price" would be.

In broad perspective, what emerged from developing countries prior to and during the Seattle meeting were proposals principally aimed at improving market access, strengthening rules, or rebalancing agreements. With respect to the rules, frequently cited concerns relate to the need to adjust the anti-dumping disciplines; the reduction of those tariffs that remain high in industrial-country markets; improved market access in agriculture;

the simplification of rules of origin; and modification of certain provisions of the Subsidies Agreement and the Trade-Related Aspects of Intellectual Property Rights Agreement. Developing countries have called for a fundamental reassessment of special and differential treatment provisions, especially in some agreements such as the Technical Barriers to Trade and the Sanitary and Phyto-Sanitary Agreements and the Customs Valuation Agreement, as well as mandatory "best endeavor" provisions for industrial countries to provide sufficient technical assistance, adjustment finance, and technology transfer. Addressing these areas constructively will facilitate the dialogue on trade and environmental issues. So, too, would offering assurances to developing countries that proposals to enforce labor standards with trade sanctions are off the table.

Another constructive initiative would be to launch a greatly improved program to build the human and institutional capacity of developing countries to enable their delegations to participate fully in multilateral negotiations with the appropriate depth of support in national capitals.[2] Many of these national delegations in Geneva are small or nonexistent, and the countries do not have the appropriate resources at home to service the negotiating process and participate effectively. This can only come about with a strengthening of the human and institutional capacity to service the WTO process. This, in turn, is only possible if resources are made available for technical assistance and training. In this respect, the funds earmarked for technical assistance in the regular WTO budget are but a drop in the ocean.

It is important to enhance the regular budget of the WTO to greatly increase the technical assistance resources available for developing countries. At the same time, a coherent and integrated effort on the part of all relevant international organizations must be given high priority if developing countries are to have the necessary capacity to engage in and benefit from future negotiations. This is particularly the case for the least developed countries, which are still awaiting the benefits of an open and liberal rules-based multilateral trading system.

. . . .

CONSULTATION WITH CIVIL SOCIETY

■   THERE IS GENERAL AGREEMENT THAT THE AIRING of views made possible through the WTO symposia described in Chapter 3 has provided a valuable channel of communication among governments, NGOs, and international organizations. Nevertheless, the productivity and the impact of the meetings could be greatly improved. In particular, the interests of the NGOs at the meetings are characteristically very diverse. As only plenary sessions have been held during the symposia, much of the discussion was not of interest to some participants. The meetings could be much more effective if participants were to address specific issues in a far more detailed manner, concentrating on the nature of the perceived problems and the proposals. This could be done through discussions in workshops, where a higher degree of specificity would be possible.

For WTO members to hear a representative selection of views, it is important that a cross section of the environmental NGO community be represented. This includes small NGOs, sometimes from the least developed countries. These representatives seldom have the resources to participate in such meetings. Including them in the meetings requires a budget. WTO members have left it to the Secretariat to find funds for these meetings, as they have not been prepared to provide for the symposia in the regular WTO budget. Chasing funding has been time-consuming and an inefficient use of what are already strained Secretariat resources. Resources have been provided through the generosity of a small number of countries (in particular, the Netherlands, Canada, and the Nordic countries) but some larger countries—frequently the most vocal ones in claiming support for NGO involvement—provide the least funds, or none at all. A good gesture and practical initiative would be for WTO members to agree to fund future symposia through the regular WTO budget.

As with the symposia, the highly successful regional seminars also described in Chapter 3 were financed outside the regular budget of the WTO. Despite the enthusiasm of developing country (as well as industrial country) officials for these meetings, they have been abandoned because of lack of funding.

. . . .

TRANSPARENCY

■ ONE CALL THAT IS COMMON FROM ALL NGOs (and others) is for a more open and transparent WTO. Much has been already been done in improving the transparency and public knowledge about the WTO. Many have been concerned that opening up the organization could adversely affect its intergovernmental character. These concerns have proved to be misplaced. But more still needs to be done to improve the transparency of the WTO.

With respect to the derestriction of documents, there is no reason why all WTO documents should not be publicly circulated at the time governments receive them. The only exceptions should be those that contain genuine secrets or where public access to their contents would jeopardize the negotiating position of individual members. As very few documents could be considered confidential according to this criteria, almost all documents should be circulated as derestricted. Procedures for delayed derestriction should only apply to WTO activities in which there is a strong case for maintaining a period of confidentiality while an issue is subject to consideration by WTO bodies. For these documents, derestriction should come only when the information is no longer confidential (such as documents containing tariff offers in liberalization negotiations, or confidential information on the status of balance-of-payments).[3]

As far as distribution is concerned, these documents should be available on the WTO Web site. Considerable progress has been made in this area in recent years in line with technological developments. For example, all national submissions with respect to the proposed agenda and other substantive and procedural considerations relating to the Seattle ministerial meeting were made publicly available (through a posting on the WTO home page) as soon as time and resources permitted. This would have been inconceivable in even the recent past. There have been no apparent adverse effects.

On this basis, Secretariat background notes, minutes, and agendas of meetings should be derestricted when they are circulated to governments. Some members maintain that minutes and any formal summaries of meetings should be derestricted only after three months, to allow time to ensure that delegations have been correctly quoted. Misquotations are rare, however, and a correction can always be issued. In addition, these small inconveniences are far outweighed by the benefits of a well-informed public. Documents relating to the Trade Policy Review Mechanism should continue to be subject to current procedures, which already provide for derestriction upon expiration of the press embargo. National submissions should be made available immediately, unless national interests would somehow be adversely affected.[4]

Many would like to have more rapid access to the findings of the panels. In Chapter 3, the practical considerations relating to the timing of the availability of panel reports were addressed. Panel reports could be made available more rapidly in three ways. The first is to make the panel report available immediately after it is out in whatever the working language of the panel had been (in most cases, English). A second option would be to distribute only the findings of the panel (which interest the public) in the working languages and not wait for the summaries of the argumentation to be available in all working languages (as is the current practice). In the shrimp-turtle case, the panel findings were just 20 pages long and the panel conclusions only 2 pages, whereas the full report was 431 tightly written, single-spaced pages. The third solution would be to provide the Secretariat with the resources to produce the full report more quickly. (The same options could apply to Appellate Body reports.)

· ·

PUBLIC ACCESS

■   AS FAR AS ACCESS TO THE WTO "PROCESS" is concerned, most NGOs do not appear to be seeking a role in the negotiations at the multilateral level. Even if they were, it is clear that WTO members would not agree to this. The desire to have access to the process is presumably driven by a desire to be better informed and to influence the negotiating process itself. Improved access to information through the accelerated derestriction of documents will certainly help. Influencing the negotiating process, however, should be done at the national level through public debate. Nevertheless, a case can be made for giving environmental groups a chance to make their concerns known at the multilateral level. This need not be viewed as lobbying per se, but rather as conveying what should be considered useful information to assist negotiators in taking decisions that are more in line with public thinking.

One approach could be to create a subgroup of the Committee on Trade and the Environment (CTE) where government officials and NGOs could meet regularly, discuss issues, consider proposals, and report their findings back to the full committee. This would be institutionally difficult to achieve, as it would require formal approval of members. A less formal approach that would have the same effect could be to build on the experience of the symposia organized by the WTO Secretariat. At these meetings, NGOs have interacted directly with WTO members. These symposia should be institutionalized and allocated a budget by WTO members; they could continue to be held back-to-back with meetings of the CTE. The relevance of this process would be increased if the two meetings had similar agendas. Summary records of the symposia proceedings could be prepared and made publicly available. This has in fact been done in the past.[5] The proceedings have been widely available through the Internet and elsewhere, including on the WTO Web site. What is lacking is a formal channel of communication of the ideas and concerns presented in the symposia to governments. To meet this end, a report on the proceedings of the symposia could be forwarded to the CTE by an independent moderator nominated for the occasion. It could be done by the Director-General of the WTO (or a nominated official), or by the Chairman of the CTE.

Past practice would indicate that this could be done immediately and would not necessarily require the approval of members, as a precedent does exist. The Deputy Director-General of the WTO made such a report to the CTE following the WTO/NGO symposium of 1998. No government objected to this approach, and the discussions in the CTE that followed the symposium (and that are recorded in the summary records of the meeting) very much reflected the concerns expressed by the participants in the symposium itself.

. . . .

COOPERATION WITH OTHER
INTERNATIONAL ORGANIZATIONS

■   IT SHOULD BE POSSIBLE TO ENHANCE TRANSPARENCY, dialogue, and cooperation between representatives of multilateral environmental agreements (MEAs), relevant international organizations, and the WTO from the initial stage of negotiation of an MEA to its implementation. This cooperation may include exchange of information, mutual participation in meetings, access to documents and databases, and briefing sessions, as necessary. It has been proposed in the CTE that a guide containing WTO principles could be compiled by the Secretariat that could be used by MEA negotiators in their consideration of proposed trade measures.

There could be cooperation agreements between the WTO and MEA institutions providing for the WTO Secretariat to respond to requests for technical information about relevant WTO provisions. Representatives of the MEAs could continue to regularly address the CTE and inform them of relevant aspects of their agreements and recent developments in negotiations.

. . . .

ROLE OF THE CTE IN
LIBERALIZATION NEGOTIATIONS

■ THERE HAS BEEN A GREAT DEAL OF DISCUSSION about the link between trade liberalization and the environment, and about sectors where trade liberalization could improve the environment. The important question is how to bring this work to a conclusion with policy implications. From a practical perspective, most of the work has been done at the sectoral level, yet this is not where negotiations for the removal of trade restrictions takes place. It occurs at a far more disaggregated level—in fact, frequently at the tariff line level. Products now need to be identified within sectors to permit liberalization negotiations to proceed.

The WTO Secretariat could play a role in this respect, but the most productive way forward would be for individual governments to propose specific products to the CTE that are a priority for them. This is not an unreasonable expectation, because some governments have already announced their priority sectors and done considerable work in justifying their claims.[6] More proposals should be encouraged from both industrial and developing countries, based on their national experiences.

In collecting this information, there is a real opportunity for NGOs to work constructively with WTO members. Their local knowledge of the environmental implications of trade restrictions and distortions far exceeds that of trade officials, even if NGOs do not necessarily view environmental problems in terms of trade restrictions. The potential for useful work in this area has become apparent in the success NGOs have had in drawing attention to the fact that WTO may be able to take action regarding environmentally harmful fisheries subsidies. This has spawned a series of publications, proposals, and meetings to address the issue.

The bottom line, however, is that liberalization negotiations will only take place if WTO members call for them, and the CTE is not a committee where trade liberalization will be negotiated or discussed in an operational sense. This would encroach on the work of other committees dealing directly with market access, agriculture, subsidies, and so on. But this does not preclude the committee from making recommendations in this area in the form of a decision or declaration regarding the priorities for action elsewhere in the WTO from an environmental perspective. There will, for example, be negotiations on removing trade restrictions and distortions in agriculture in accordance with the Agreement on Agriculture, even with the failure in Seattle. Although many governments maintain that fish and fish products are a priority for negotiations on environmental grounds, these are specifically excluded from the negotiations. The CTE could recommend how to deal with the fishery sector in future negotiations. In fact, making recommendations is what the CTE is mandated to do. As noted in Chapter 2, a lack of recommendations is one of the principal criticisms leveled at the CTE.[7]

The usefulness of this approach is underscored by the fact that there are clear advantages for developing countries under this agenda item of the CTE, whereas none are seen elsewhere. Similarly, given the strength of feeling in the NGO community about some of the areas where the environment could be positively affected—particularly fisheries—it would be a clear and tangible indication to them that the WTO was prepared to work in a coherent manner with them and other international organizations (such as the U.N. Environment Programme and the U.N. Food and Agriculture Organization) in matters relating to the environment.

There must be close coordination between ministries at the national level for such an initiative to be effective. National representatives working in areas such as agriculture and subsidies should coordinate with their counterparts dealing with trade and the environment. It is likely that agriculture negotiators would be unhappy if their colleagues in the CTE provided information about the environmental degradation associated with agricultural trade restrictions and distortions, as this could upset their own negotiating strategies. Viewed constructively, however, such a declaration coming from the CTE should stiffen the backbone of national negotiators taking decisions that may adversely affect some interest groups but that are in the interests of the community at large.

It should be borne in mind, however, that trade expansion—whether through liberalization or any other means—can result in environmental damage through an intensification of what are inappropriate resource usage and consumption patterns. It is time for a formal recognition on the part of WTO members that this may be the case, and that what is needed is the coordination of efforts to ensure that the appropriate environmental management policies are adopted so that trade expansion is not harmful to the environment and supports sustainable development.

. . . .

THE CTE AND
SUSTAINABLE DEVELOPMENT

■ THE WORK OF THE CTE HAS BEEN USEFUL in gaining a greater understanding of many of the complex issues in the trade and environment debate (see Chapter 2). After five years of meetings, however, it is time to reconsider if there is still a role for the committee and, if so, what that role should be. This could be done by asking what work remains to be done to complete the mandate given to the CTE by ministers in Marrakesh. The answer is that probably very little needs to be done in the sense of identifying the problems associated with the various agenda items as well as proposals for dealing with them. This does not mean, however, that there is not a need to keep the issues under review.

Although no problems have arisen with respect to coherence between WTO rules and MEAs, for example, this is not to say that they will not arise in the future. It has been argued in Chapter 6 that this may well be the case for the Biosafety Protocol and the Kyoto Protocol, for example. It is more important than ever to have a forum for an exchange of views between representatives of the various MEAs and WTO members. There would be no other forum if the CTE did not exist. Similarly, the useful work on identifying win-win possibilities appears to be reaching a stage where positive results may emerge. It would be unfortunate if this work were not taken further, with recommendations being made by the Committee.

Reviewing what still needs to be done to complete the work program of the CTE would provide the possibility for the agenda to be given greater relevance in the light of the past work of the committee. It would also provide the possibility to introduce new items and modify the agenda as a result of changes in priorities over the last five years. In short, the work of the committee could be made more relevant. As noted earlier, for example, it could become the channel of communication for the concerns of environmentalists through regular meetings held back to back with symposia for NGOs, government officials, and international organizations. Various delegations have proposed "mainstreaming" environmental issues by factoring these concerns into the WTO across the board. In this scenario, each relevant WTO committee would deal with environment under its area of authority. Although this may hold some appeal—particularly for large delegations—it is difficult to see how mainstreaming could be carried out in practice. Resources devoted by governments to questions relating to the environment are already spread thinly in WTO meetings. This is evidenced, for example, by the small number of developing-country delegations that are active in the CTE. Mainstreaming may just lead to a dilution of already inadequate resources and a further minimization of attention paid to trade and environmental issues.

Nevertheless, there will certainly be a need to monitor the manner in which environmental concerns are dealt with in the various negotiating groups should broad-based negotiations be launched in the coming years. In this respect there is an important role for the CTE. It could, for example, provide a forum for countries that choose to review trade and environment linkages of the negotiations. It could also provide the focal point for the identification and discussion of links among the various elements of the negotiating agenda and the environment. This role could be further broadened if a similar mandate were given to the Committee on Trade and Development (CTD).

The CTE and the CTD could each provide a forum to identify and debate the developmental and environmental aspects of the negotiations, including the synergies between trade liberalization, economic development, and environmental protection. The work of the two bodies would be complementary and would help ensure that the negotiations are in line with the preamble of the WTO agreement by acting in accordance with the objectives of sustainable development and responding to the needs of developing countries, especially the least-developed ones.

. . . .

STANDARDS AND LABELING

■   THE CHALLENGE FACING WTO MEMBERS in implementing various agreements is to provide the necessary flexibility for governments to pursue the domestic policies they think are appropriate without the associated measures being used as disguised barriers to trade. According to WTO agreements, members should be guided by scientific principles when deciding the appropriate level of protection, so that the decisions are not arbitrary or protectionist. In other international and national agreements, precaution in the absence of science plays a far larger role, placing WTO rules on a collision course with a number of national regulations and international agreements. If the WTO finds itself an adjudicator in areas where the public feels passionately one way or the other (and in the absence of scientific evidence), its credibility will certainly be at stake.

There is no easy answer to this problem. It is clear, however, that the WTO should not be the arbitrator on matters well outside the realm of conventional trade policy considerations without this position being agreed to in advance. It is not reasonable to expect to find solutions requiring multilateral agreement in the case of disputes involving food safety or protection of endangered species that cannot be settled bilaterally. Nor should the problem be relegated to a dispute settlement process where trade officials on a de facto basis take decisions that will almost by definition (because there is no agreement at the national level) be unpopular with large parts of the public. The way to deal with the problem must be discussed in the context of policy choices relating to the use of the precautionary principle. There must be a coherent approach to dealing with problems where scientific evidence alone does not make the policy choices clear.

The way to deal with the precautionary principle from a trade policy perspective should be addressed directly. This should be done at two levels. First, it is important to take account of the fact that the precautionary principle is applied in each instance on a case-by-case basis. The facts surrounding the perceived need to take action in the absence of scientific evidence are different in the case of climate change, loss of biodiversity, and trade in genetically modified organisms (GMOs). When the need arises, a working group could be established to deal with the specific case in question. Not surprisingly, a working group on biotechnology has already been proposed with a fact-finding mandate to consider the adequacy and effectiveness of existing rules as well as the capacity of WTO members to implement these rules. It would be useful to establish guidelines according to which such groups could be established. It should be useful to reach agreement on principles that would guide the establishment of such groups and ensure that their work is consistent with that being undertaken elsewhere. In the case of biotechnology, for example, it was clear in Seattle that many WTO members and public interest groups are concerned that a WTO working group could undermine negotiations on the January 2000 Biosafety Protocol to the Convention on Biological Diversity.

Closely related to standards is the condition under which a WTO member can legally label a product according to how it was manufactured. When preferences differ between consumers for nonscientific reasons—that is, products are physically the same or like products—one approach is to permit consumers to differentiate through reference to product labels. The WTO rules that apply to labeling are quite unclear at a time when labeling is increasingly likely to be an issue in the coming years for goods with enormous commercial value. They should be clarified as a priority. The uncertainty that surrounds their application will bring unpredictability to commercial operations—the very thing the WTO was designed to avoid. Here, too, individual cases differ according to circumstances, and while a general clarification of rules would be useful, it is important to consider individual instances. The issues raised with respect to labeling of products derived from GMOs and those relating to the labor conditions under which a good (or service) differ greatly and should be treated separately. The proposal relating to the establishment of a Working Party on Biotechnology, for example, envisages specifically addressing labeling issues.

At a second level, many of the issues related to the application of the precautionary principle touch on ethical and other considerations. Deciding how to deal with these matters in the WTO should not be left to negotiators working according to briefs that reflect only national interests. What is at stake is maintaining the effective operation of the multilateral trading system while dealing with concerns that go far beyond conventional trade policy. To do this, the choices should be referred to a group of eminent persons to look at the broader question of the role of the WTO in global governance. This proposal is discussed at the end of this chapter.

. . . .

MULTILATERAL ENVIRONMENTAL AGREEMENTS

■   MULTILATERAL ENVIRONMENTAL AGREEMENTS (MEAs) provide a safeguard against unilateral attempts to address environmental problems.

Unilateral solutions are often discriminatory and frequently involve the extraterritorial application of values and environmental standards. The Earth Summit in 1992 clearly endorsed consensual and cooperative multilateral environmental solutions to global environmental problems. These reduce the risks of arbitrary discrimination and disguised protectionism, and reflect the international community's common concern and responsibility for global resources. But the rules of multilateral trade and environmental agreements need to be consistent. Improved policy coordination at the national level between trade and environmental policy officials can contribute substantially to eliminating policy conflicts.

It would also seem appropriate to create a "framework" within which MEAs can operate more effectively so that environmental problems can be dealt with outside the WTO. In developing such a framework, the first order of business must be reaching consensus on the standards according to which there can be discrimination in trade for products that are physically the same, or which products should not enter international trade. This can and has been done in a variety of MEAs. Few would disagree about the need for restrictions on trade in stolen goods, and that they should be regulated in a discriminatory fashion, even if the physical form of the goods is the same. But few would argue that solutions to these sorts of problems are within the competence of the WTO.

The same is true with matters relating to the environment, as environmental standards for agreed production and process methods and products could be set by experts. If there are grounds for discrimination in trade because of the characteristics of what is being traded (endangered species) or how a product is produced (carbon-emitting production processes), the appropriate standards should be established through agreement by government experts. As this procedure would relieve the WTO of many concerns relating to difficult concepts such as like products and non-product-related product and production methods, it is not surprising that WTO members as well as panel and appellate body reports have strongly promoted the use of multilateral or other agreements to deal with these matters.

If the agreed solution involves a loss of rights under the WTO (that is, being discriminated against), then providing all WTO members agree to forgo those rights, it is difficult to see where there could be a problem. A "framework" could formalize this reality. The framework could also make clear that if the membership of the MEA coincides with that of the WTO, then disputes over a trade measure used for environmental purposes in accordance with the MEA should be dealt with through the MEA compliance mechanism.

Problems arise if there is not a common membership between the WTO and an MEA. In this respect, the critical question is: if an exception is sought in the WTO for a nonconforming measure taken in accordance with an MEA, what support should be given to the government seeking the exception due to the existence of the MEA? The answer is very clear: it depends. The framework should contain a procedure whereby this question is addressed on a multilateral basis with the involvement of both the trade and environmental communities; it should not be left in the hands of panelists in the WTO dispute settlement process or the appellate body. In fact, the decision could be taken through a public debate and disclosure of all the relevant facts. At the most fundamental level, what is required is a coherent approach to the formulation of trade and environmental policies at both the national and the multilateral level. Greater coherence between multilateral trade agreements and MEAs could be best achieved by establishing a group to examine the question, as discussed below.

. . . .

DISPUTE SETTLEMENT

■ IT HAS BEEN PROPOSED DURING DISCUSSIONS of the WTO review of the Dispute Settlement Body process that the consultative stage be strengthened. The justification for this has been largely in terms of relieving the panel caseload. But a modified approach to the consultative process could have other advantages, a number of which could well address the concerns of NGOs and directly address the criticisms of a lack of openness and participation of civil society.

Although it is impossible to predict the political acceptability of the idea, it may be worth considering public debate in the case of environmental disputes. A moderator could be nominated by the Director-General to hear all sides and propose a solution. This could be done in a totally transparent manner with inputs from technical experts. A reading of the shrimp-turtle appellate body report, for example, leads to the conclusion that this dispute should not have come to the WTO. In its simplest terms, the appellate body found that agreement should have been sought and reached on a regional basis. Threatening the credibility of the multilateral trading system—as directly addressed by the panelists in the shrimp-turtle dispute—would never have been an issue.

Creating the possibility of public hearings with a moderator would not be an obligation imposed on disputing parties. The option of requesting the good offices of the Director-General for formal consultations, as provided for in the Dispute Settlement Understanding, would remain open. It is worth noting that in the shrimp-turtle case, the good offices of the Director-General were not sought. Nor are they in most cases. If it were thought that a public hearing would delay a process that could be urgent from an environmental perspective, it could be counterargued that the absence of a formal procedure would expedite the process and if there were no definitive outcome, presumably the consultations under the good offices of the Director-General would not be required. In any event, special procedures could be developed to deal with emergency situations.

Even if there were not a positive outcome in terms of a clear decision, this process would be totally transparent—something sought by many representatives of civil society. The possibility of providing inputs from technical experts is another advantage. And the more formal disputes settlement process would be avoided if the mediation were successful, although the normal channel of disputes settlement would still remain open. No country's rights and obligations would be affected in this process, but it could be argued that the technical information provided could eventually influence the conclusion of the panel or the appellate body, if the process went that far. Yet it is hard to argue that additional factual information is a handicap if a well-informed decision is the ultimate objective.

But what is so special about environmental disputes that an approach such as this is warranted? Nothing. The process is equally applicable to all potential disputes if the defending and complaining countries agree. Indeed, such a process could be established outside the WTO if the idea were not adopted there and would greatly relieve the pressure on WTO resources.

SPECIAL REVIEW GROUPS

■ BASED ON EXPERIENCE IN THE URUGUAY ROUND, it would seem appropriate to consider creating at least two groups to deal with problems relating to trade and the environment.

In the Uruguay Round, a group was set up to review the Articles of the GATT. The outcome of this process was a series of understandings relating to individual articles to clarify their application in the light of four decades of experience. In this process, the exceptions provision of GATT (Article XX) was examined and no change thought necessary. But times may have changed. Given the discussion in recent years and the controversy over the interpretation of the exceptions provisions, it is appropriate to consider if an understanding or an interpretation is now required. As many of the matters involved in the Article XX disputes have been of considerable importance from a policy perspective, it is far preferable to give priority to the GATT/WTO tradition of deciding policy through debate and consensus rather letting policy evolve through litigation.

A second group could be established to bring coherence between multilateral trade and multilateral environmental policies. Here, too, a precedent exists. In the Uruguay Round, a group was created to examine ways to bring greater coherence to global economic policymaking. The so-called FOGS Group (Functioning of the GATT System) produced a Ministerial Declaration on the Contribution of the World Trade Organization to Achieving Greater Coherence in Global Economic Policymaking. Ministers recognized that "difficulties, the origins of which lie outside the trade field can not be redressed through measures taken in the trade field alone." They acknowledged that the "interlinkages between the different aspects of economic policy require that the international institutions with responsibilities in each of these areas follow consistent and mutually supportive policies."[8]

As the declaration called for the WTO to develop cooperation with other international organizations, it served as the basis for the comprehensive and formal agreements that were struck between the WTO, the World Bank, and the International Monetary Fund. Although the FOGS Group concentrated on bringing greater coherence to economic policymaking, it would seem reasonable that a similar group give guidance as to how to establish a mutually supportive relationship between the WTO and various

environmental agreements. This could well be the objective of a FOWTOG—
a Functioning of the World Trade Organization Group.

· ·

THE WTO AND GLOBAL GOVERNANCE

■   THE TIME HAS COME TO CONSIDER A WAY to deal with a number of
the problems of a systemic nature described in the foregoing chapters.
This could be done outside the negotiating context and by those with the
capacity to adopt a broader vision of the role of the world trading system in
global governance.

A fundamental question that such a group could address is when
can trade measures be used to discriminate between like products made with
different production processes. The answer to this question is relevant in
ethical matters such as defining the role of precaution in the absence of
scientific evidence and the use of unilateral trade measures to enforce nationally preferred environmental standards. It also underpins the concerns of
developing countries with respect to the eventual inclusion of matters
relating to labor standards, and a new "justification" for protection on
moral grounds.

Unlike other international institutions, the WTO has had extremely
limited recourse to High Level or Eminent Persons Groups. One exception
has been the Leutwiler Group, which addressed a number of systemic issues
prior to the launching of the Uruguay Round and issued an influential report
entitled "Trade Policies for a Better Future: Proposals for Action."[9] Few
would deny the important contribution of this group to the Uruguay Round
negotiations in terms of new policy orientations.[10] Their view was that
"governments should be required regularly to explain and defend their overall trade policies. . . . the making of trade policy should be brought into the
open. The costs and benefits of trade policy actions existing and prospective
should be analyzed through a 'protection balance sheet.' Public support for
open trade policies should be fostered."[11] The outcome of the proposals of
the group for greater transparency was the creation of the Trade Policy
Review Mechanism at the Montreal ministerial meeting in 1988.

The WTO has extended its reach far beyond that of GATT, and its
importance in international economic and political affairs has increased

dramatically as a result. For this reason alone it would be timely for a group of eminent persons to take stock of the role of the WTO in world economic and political affairs. But the real rationale for a Group of Eminent Persons does not lie here. It is rather to address the role of the WTO in global governance in the new millennium. Nothing more, nothing less. There seem to be expectations that the WTO should deal with matters relating to economic, social, ethical, and cultural issues. Perhaps it should and can. If this is the case, then it merits discussion by competent people outside the normal rough and tumble of trade negotiations.

NOTES

[1] See Magda Shahin, "Trade and Environment; How Real is the Debate," in Gary P. Sampson and W. Bradnee Chambers (eds.), *Trade, Environment and the Millennium* (Tokyo: United Nations University Press, 1999).

[2] In the case of trade negotiations, for example, while the participation of developing countries in WTO negotiations has increased greatly, so has the frequency, complexity, and resource intensity of the negotiations. As noted in Chapter 2, 25 developing countries took part in the Kennedy Round of negotiations in 1964–67, 68 in the Tokyo Round in 1973–79, and 76 in the Uruguay Round in 1986–94. There are currently more than 100 developing-country members of the WTO.

[3] These would include documents relating to Working Parties on Accession (documents submitted by the acceding country could be subject to earlier derestriction if the acceding country so indicates to the secretariat), documents relating to balance-of-payments consultations, and documents relating to the Budget Committee.

[4] This would include documents in the Secret/series (that is, documents relating to Article XXVIII negotiations, including processes initiated pursuant to Article XXIV:6).

[5] To maintain its independence, the WTO Secretariat has commissioned the International Institute for Sustainable Development to prepare these records.

[6] Examples include the U.S. and New Zealand papers on fisheries, the Colombian paper on cut flowers, and the Brazilian paper on ethanol as an environmentally friendly product. These are all formal submissions to the CTE.

[7] See WTO Secretariat, *Environmental Benefits of Removing Trade Restrictions and Distortions*, WT/CTE/W/67 (Geneva: WTO, 8 November 1997).

[8] See WTO, "Declaration on the Contribution of the WTO to Achieving Greater Coherence in Global Economic Policyamaking," in *The Results of the Uruguay Round of Multilateral Trade Negotiations: The Legal Text* (Geneva: WTO, 1994).

[9] Leutwiler Report, *Trade Policies for a Better Future: Proposals for Action* (Geneva: GATT Secretariat, 1985).

Trade-Related Environmental Disputes[1]

Under the GATT, six panel proceedings involving an examination of environmental measures or human health-related measures under Article XX were completed. Of the six reports, three have not been adopted. Under the WTO Dispute Settlement Understanding, two such proceedings have been completed. The following provides a factual overview of these disputes.

(1) UNITED STATES—PROHIBITION ON THE IMPORTS OF TUNA AND TUNA PRODUCTS FROM CANADA, ADOPTED ON 22 FEBRUARY 1982

An import prohibition was introduced by the United States after Canada had seized 19 fishing vessels and arrested U.S. fishermen fishing for albacore tuna, without authorization from the Canadian government, in waters considered by Canada to be under its jurisdiction. The United States did not recognize this jurisdiction and introduced an import prohibition to retaliate under the Fishery Conservation and Management Act.

The Panel found that the import prohibition was contrary to Article XI:1, and was justified neither under Article XI:2, nor under Article XX(g) of the General Agreement.

(2) CANADA—MEASURES AFFECTING EXPORTS OF UNPROCESSED HERRING AND SALMON, ADOPTED ON 22 MARCH 1988

Under the 1976 Canadian Fisheries Act, Canada maintained regulations prohibiting the exportation or sale for export of certain unprocessed herring and salmon. The United States complained that these measures were inconsistent with GATT Article XI. Canada argued that these export restrictions were part of a system of fishery resource management aimed at preserving fish stocks, and therefore were justified under Article XX(g).

The Panel found that the measures maintained by Canada were contrary GATT Article XI:1 and were justified neither by Article XI:2(b) nor by Article XX(g).

(3) THAILAND—RESTRICTIONS ON THE IMPORTATION OF AND INTERNAL TAXES ON CIGARETTES, ADOPTED ON 7 NOVEMBER 1990

Under the 1966 Tobacco Act, Thailand prohibited the importation of cigarettes and other tobacco preparations, but authorized the sale of domestic cigarettes; moreover, cigarettes were subject to an excise tax, a business tax, and a municipal tax. The United States complained that the import restrictions were inconsistent with GATT Article XI:1 and considered that they were justified neither by Article XI:2(c), nor by Article XX(b). It also argued that the internal taxes were inconsistent with GATT Article III:2. Thailand argued, inter alia, that the import restrictions were justified under Article XX(b) because the government had adopted measures which could only be effective if cigarette imports were prohibited and because chemicals and other additives contained in U.S. cigarettes might make them more harmful than Thai cigarettes.

The Panel found that the import restrictions were inconsistent with Article XI:1 and not justified under Article X1:2(c). It further concluded that the import restrictions were not "necessary" within the meaning of Article XX(b). The internal taxes were found to be consistent with Article III:2.

(4) UNITED STATES—RESTRICTIONS ON THE IMPORTS OF TUNA, NOT ADOPTED, CIRCULATED ON 3 SEPTEMBER 1991

The Marine Mammal Protection Act (MMPA) required a general prohibition of the "taking" (harassment, hunting, capture, killing, or attempt thereof) and importation into the United States of marine mammals, except with explicit authorization. It governed, in particular, the taking of marine mammals incidental to harvesting yellowfin tuna in the Eastern Tropical Pacific Ocean (ETP), an area where dolphins are known to swim above schools of tuna. Under the MMPA, the importation of commercial fish or products from fish which have been caught with commercial fishing technology which results in the incidental kill or incidental serious injury of ocean mammals in excess of U.S. standards were prohibited.

In particular, the importation of yellowfin tuna harvested with purse-seine nets in the ETP was prohibited (primary nation embargo), unless the competent U.S. authorities established that (i) the government of the harvesting country had a programme regulating the taking of marine mammals, comparable to that of the United States, and (ii) the average rate of incidental taking of marine mammals by vessels of the harvesting nation was comparable to the average rate of such taking by U.S. vessels. The average incidental taking rate (in terms of dolphins killed each time in the purse-seine nets are set) for that country's tuna fleet were not to exceed 1.25 times the average taking rate of U.S. vessels in the same period. Imports of tuna from countries purchasing tuna from a country subject to the primary nation embargo were also prohibited (intermediary nation embargo).

Mexico claimed that the import prohibition on yellowfin tuna and tuna products was inconsistent with Articles XI, XIII, and III of GATT. The United States requested the Panel to find that the direct embargo was consistent with Article III and, in the alternative, was covered by Articles XX(b) and XX(g). The United States also argued that the intermediary nation embargo was consistent with Article III and, in the alternative, was justified by Article XX, paragraphs (b), (d), and (g).

The Panel found that the import prohibition under the direct and the intermediary embargoes did not constitute internal regulations within the meaning of Article III, was inconsistent with Article XI:1, and was not justified by Article XX paragraphs (b) and (g). Moreover, the intermediary embargo was not justified under Article XX(d).

(5) UNITED STATES—RESTRICTIONS OF THE IMPORTS OF TUNA, NOT ADOPTED, CIRCULATED ON 16 JUNE 1994

The EEC and the Netherlands complained that both the primary and the intermediary nation embargoes, enforced pursuant to the MMPA (see above paragraph 7), did not fall under Article III, were inconsistent with Article XI:1, and were not covered by any of the exceptions of Article XX. The United States considered that the intermediary nation embargo was consistent with GATT since it was covered by Article XX, paragraphs (g), (b), and (d), and that the primary nation embargo did not nullify or impair any benefits accruing to the EEC or the Netherlands since it did not apply to these countries.

The Panel found that neither the primary nor the intermediary nation embargo were covered under Article III, that both were contrary to Article XI:1 and not covered by the exceptions in Article XX (b), (g), or (d) of the GATT.

(6) UNITED STATES—TAXES ON AUTOMOBILES, NOT ADOPTED, CIRCULATED ON 11 OCTOBER 1994

Three U.S. measures on automobiles were under examination: the luxury tax on automobiles ("luxury tax"), the gas guzzler tax on automobiles ("gas guzzler"), and the Corporate Average Fuel Economy regulation ("CAFE"). The European Community complained that these measures were inconsistent with GATT Article III and could not be justified under Article XX(g) or (d). The United States considered that these measures were consistent with the General Agreement.

The Panel found that both the luxury tax—which applied to cars sold for over $30,000—and the gas guzzler tax—which applied to the sale of automobiles attaining less than 22.5 miles per gallon (mpg)—were consistent with Article III:2 of GATT.

The CAFE regulation required the average fuel economy for passenger cars manufactured in the United States or sold by any importer not to fall below 27.5 mpg. Companies that were both importers and domestic manufacturers had to calculate average fuel economy separately for imported passenger automobiles and for those manufactured domestically. The Panel found the CAFE regulation to be inconsistent with GATT Article III:4 because the separate foreign fleet accounting system discriminated against foreign cars and the fleet averaging differentiated between imported and domestic cars on the basis of factors relating to control or ownership of producers or importers, rather than on the basis of factors directly related to the products as such. Similarly, the Panel found that the separate foreign fleet accounting was not justified under Article XX(g); it did not make a finding on the consistency of the fleet averaging method with Article XX(g). The Panel found that the CAFE regulation could not be justified under Article XX(d).

(7) UNITED STATES—STANDARDS FOR REFORMULATED AND CONVENTIONAL GASOLINE, ADOPTED ON 20 MAY 1996

Following a 1990 amendment to the Clean Air Act, the Environmental Protection Agency (EPA) promulgated the Gasoline Rule on the composition and emissions effects of gasoline, in order to reduce air pollution in the United States. From 1 January 1995, the Gasoline Rule permitted only gasoline of a specified cleanliness ("reformulated gasoline") to be sold to consumers in the most polluted areas of the country. In the rest of the country, only gasoline no dirtier than that sold in the base year of 1990 ("conventional gasoline") could be sold. The Gasoline Rule applied to all U.S. refiners, blenders, and importers of gasoline. It required any domestic refiner which was in operation for at least 6 months in 1990 to establish an individual refinery baseline, which represented the quality of gasoline produced by that refiner in 1990. EPA also established a statutory baseline, intended to reflect average U.S. 1990 gasoline quality. The statutory baseline was assigned to those refiners who were not in operation for at least six months in 1990 and to importers and blenders of gasoline. Compliance with the baselines was measured on an average annual basis.

Venezuela and Brazil claimed that the Gasoline Rule was inconsistent, inter alia, with GATT Article III, and was not covered by Article XX. The United States argued that the Gasoline Rule was consistent with Article III and, in any event, was justified under the exceptions contained in GATT Article XX, paragraphs (b), (g), and (d).

The Panel found that the Gasoline Rule was inconsistent with Article III and could not be justified under paragraphs (b), (d), or (g). On appeal of the Panel's findings on Article XX(g), the Appellate Body found that the baseline establishment rules contained in the Gasoline Rule fell within the terms of Article XX(g) but failed to meet the requirements of the chapeau of Article XX.

(8) UNITED STATES—IMPORT PROHIBITION OF CERTAIN SHRIMP AND SHRIMP PRODUCTS, CIRCULATED ON 15 MAY 1998

In early 1997, India, Malaysia, Pakistan, and Thailand brought a joint complaint against a ban imposed by the United States on the importation of certain shrimp and shrimp products. Under U.S. legislation, wild-caught shrimp products cannot be imported in the United States if they do not meet U.S. standards regarding the protection of 5 species of sea turtles. More specifically, the United States requires that shrimp trawlers install a "turtle excluder device" (TED)[2] in their nets when fishing in areas where there is a significant likelihood of encountering sea turtles; countries wishing to export their shrimp products to the United States must impose the same requirement on their fishermen.

The Panel sought expert advice with respect to the factual aspects of the case (i.e., mainly those related to sea turtle conservation). The 5 experts consulted were sea turtle biologists and a fishery specialist. This procedure took place under Article 13 of the Dispute Settlement Understanding which allows panels to seek information, including technical and scientific advice, on matters relevant to the case. The Panel concluded that the ban imposed by the United States was not consistent with GATT Article XI (General elimination of quantitative restrictions) and could not be justified under GATT Article XX.

The Panel considered that, when invoking the right to derogate from other provisions of GATT 1994 on the basis of Article XX, a WTO member must not frustrate or defeat the object and purpose of the General Agreement and the WTO Agreement. In other words, a member must not abuse the exceptions contained in Article XX. Although environmental considerations are important for the interpretation of the WTO Agreements, as confirmed by the WTO Preamble, the object and purpose of the WTO remains the promotion of economic development through an open, predictable, and non-discriminatory trading system. Moreover, the WTO is based on a multilateral approach to trade issues and rejects unilateralism as a substitute for the procedures foreseen in the WTO Agreements.

The Panel noted that the measure at stake conditioned access to the U.S. market for shrimp products on the adoption by exporting members of sea turtle conservation policies that the United States considered to be comparable to its own. Such policy measures could, on their own, appear to have relatively minor impact on the multilateral trading system if adopted by one member; if, however, similar measures were to proliferate, they could raise a serious threat to the security and predictability of the WTO system. Indeed, if one member were allowed to adopt such measures, then other members would also have the right to adopt similar measures on the same subject, but with differing, or even conflicting, requirements. In such cases, it would be impossible for the exporting member to comply at the same time with multiple, conflicting policy requirements. Each of these requirements would necessitate the adoption of a policy applicable not only to export production (such as specific standards applicable only to goods exported to the country requiring them) but also to domestic production. Therefore, it would be impossible for a country to adopt one of these policies without running the risk of breaching other members' different policy requirements for the same products and, thus, being refused access to their markets.

The Panel concluded that the scope of Article XX, when read in the light of the object and purpose of the WTO Agreement, did not encompass measures whereby a member conditioned access to its market for a given product on the adoption of certain conservation policies by the exporting member(s).

The Panel noted that the issue at stake in this dispute was not the urgency of protecting sea turtles, as all the parties agreed that sea turtles needed to be protected and had implemented conservation programs for that purpose. Moreover, it was not the Panel's role to review either the desirability or necessity of members' environmental objectives on sea turtle conservation.

In 1991, a dispute between Mexico and United States regarding a U.S. embargo on the import of tuna from Mexico, caught using purse seine nets that resulted in the incidental kill of dolphins, heightened attention on the linkages between environmental protection policies and trade. Mexico appealed to GATT on the grounds that the embargo was inconsistent with the rules of international trade.

The panel ruled in favor of Mexico based on a number of different arguments. These included the fact that the U.S. embargo was aimed at regulating not the sale of a product, but rather its process of production (the mode of harvesting in this case). Under GATT rules, the panel argued, the United States was obliged to provide Mexican tuna (as a product) with a treatment no less favorable to that accorded to U.S. tuna (also as a product), regardless of how the tuna itself was harvested. The panel also observed that while GATT Contracting Parties could adopt GATT-inconsistent measures (falling under the "General Exceptions" clause of GATT Article XX) for the protection of the environment or the conservation of exhaustible natural resources, it was not clearly spelled out in the Agreement whether the resources being protected could fall outside the jurisdiction of the Party adopting the environmental controls.

To address this issue, the panel inspected the drafting history of the relevant section of Article XX and came to the conclusion that drafters only intended it to apply to the jurisdiction of the country taking the action. Other arguments were also put forward by the panel. Although the report of the panel was not adopted by CONTRACTING PARTIES, its ruling was heavily criticized by environmental groups that felt that trade rules were an obstacle to environmental protection.

NOTES

[1] This annex is excerpted from *WTO, GATT/WTO Dispute Settlement Practice relating to Article XX, Paragraphs (b), (d), and (g) of GATT,* WTO/CTE/W/53/Rev.1, 26 October 1998.

[2] A TED is a grip trapdoor installed inside a trawling net which allows shrimp to pass to the back of the net while directing sea turtles and other unintentionally caught large objects out of the net.

About the Author

GARY SAMPSON is currently Visiting Academic in the Department of International Relations at London School of Economics. He is also Senior Visiting Professor at the United Nations University in Tokyo and Professorial Fellow at the Melbourne Business School. He teaches on a regular basis at INSEAD in France.

For the twelve years prior to 1999, he was Director at the General Agreements on Tariffs and Trade and then the World Trade Organization. During the Uruguay Round, he headed the division responsible for the multilateral negotiations on trade in services. He subsequently directed a number of other divisions and was most recently Director of the Trade and Environment Division. He was also a senior official at the United Conference of Trade and Development for some years.

Professor Sampson is an economist with broad interests in the area of international economic relations. He has a particular interest in international trade and economic development. He has published widely on these issues and most recently co-edited a volume entitled *Trade, Environment and the Millennium* (United Nations University Press, 1999).

About the ODC

The Overseas Development Council (ODC) is an independent, international policy research institution based in Washington, DC, that seeks to improve decision making on multilateral cooperation in order to promote more effective development and the better management of related global problems. Its program focuses on the interrelationship of globalization and development, and improved multilateral responses to these linked challenges.

To this end, ODC provides analysis, information, and evaluation of multilateral policies, actions, and institutions; develops innovative ideas and new policy proposals; and creates opportunities for decision makers and other interested parties to participate in discussions of critical global issues and decisions.

ODC is governed by an international Board of Directors of recognized and widely respected policy leaders on multilateral development and global issues. Peter D. Sutherland is its Chairman, and John W. Sewell is ODC's President.

ODC is a private, nonprofit organization, funded by foundations, governments, and private individuals.

O | D | C

OVERSEAS DEVELOPMENT COUNCIL
1875 CONNECTICUT AVENUE, NW
SUITE 1012
WASHINGTON, DC 20009
TEL. 202-234-8701
FAX 202-745-0067
http://www.odc.org

ODC Board of Directors